An Aware Consumer

An Aware Consumer

Noteworthy Personal Experiences of an Activist

B. Vaidyanathan

Notion Press

Old No. 38, New No. 6
McNichols Road, Chetpet
Chennai - 600 031

First Published by Notion Press 2017
Copyright © B. Vaidyanathan 2017
All Rights Reserved.

ISBN 978-1-947498-28-0

This book has been published with all reasonable efforts taken to make the material error-free after the consent of the author. No part of this book shall be used, reproduced in any manner whatsoever without written permission from the author, except in the case of brief quotations embodied in critical articles and reviews.

The Author of this book is solely responsible and liable for its content including but not limited to the views, representations, descriptions, statements, information, opinions and references ["Content"]. The Content of this book shall not constitute or be construed or deemed to reflect the opinion or expression of the Publisher or Editor. Neither the Publisher nor Editor endorse or approve the Content of this book or guarantee the reliability, accuracy or completeness of the Content published herein and do not make any representations or warranties of any kind, express or implied, including but not limited to the implied warranties of merchantability, fitness for a particular purpose. The Publisher and Editor shall not be liable whatsoever for any errors, omissions, whether such errors or omissions result from negligence, accident, or any other cause or claims for loss or damages of any kind, including without limitation, indirect or consequential loss or damage arising out of use, inability to use, or about the reliability, accuracy or sufficiency of the information contained in this book.

the Consumer Protection Council was formed on 8th September, 1985. The objective was to safeguard the interests of the consumers and make them aware of their rights."

Over the years, the consumer movement in Rourkela has grown from strength to strength. Today with a membership of 600, the council is a watchdog of consumer interest playing its role as a counterpoise in a seller's market. With a conviction in the dictum—knowledge is power—the council seeks to educate the consumers on various topics of consumer interest by organising talks through eminent speakers and arranging consumer meets.

One of the issues taken up by the council was the poor TV reception in steel township due to the location of low power transmitter on the other side of Durgapur Hill Range. The matter was taken up with the Minister for Information and Broadcasting and as per the Director (Engg.), Directorate General, Doordarshan, the LPT will be shifted to a suitable site near the existing microwave tower, this year.

"We have been able to mobilise the consumers at Rourkela, create in them an awareness to unite and fight for their rights", says Mr. Vaidyanathan while narrating the initial success of the consumers movement. "But we still have a long way to go", he adds. Consumer movement is a continuous process, needing constant monitoring and vigil. Any let up or inertia can push us back to square one".

Mr. Vaidyanathan joined RSP in April '80 after completing his B.Tech. in Chemical Engineering from University of Madras. Initially, he was posted to by-products (Operation).

Later, after qualifying in Industrial Engineering, he moved to Industrial Engineering Department. He has done his graduation in Industrial Engineering from Indian Institute of Industrial Engineering, Bombay and obtained a Graduate Diploma in Management from All India Management Association.

The spirit of adventure is a part of Mr. Vaidyanathan's being. At college he was the Joint Secretary of the mountaineering club. "The most exciting moment was when we scaled the Lampton peak in the Western Ghats. The going was tough and demanded the adept use of mountaineering skills", he recalls with pride. In 1987, Mr. Vaidyanathan participated in the MRF sponsored South India Car Rally, along with his wife who was the navigator. They covered the distance of 800 kms. inspite of being novices and grossly ill equipped for such a gruelling course.

A modest, unassuming man Mr. Vaidyanathan's loquacity comes to the fore only when he is talking about consumerism. He identifies himself completely with the consumer movement.

What keeps him going?

"I have always been a maverick. Even today people consider me a nonconformist. There are moments of dejection when I feel the bouts of depression. But the interim success, a few words of encouragement, inspire me again and I begin with renewed determination. Any movement which remains confined to the four walls of your drawing room cannot succeed. One has to go out and struggle," he says.

Mr. Vaidyanathan is grateful to the Management of RSP for its encouragement and support. This has inspired him to enlarge the gamut of the council's activities. The latest addition to the repertoire is 'Advantage Consumer', the monthly magazine of the Council, edited by Mr. Vaidyanathan, and dedicated to the consumers' interests.

Right now, Mr. Vaidyanathan's hands are full and his problem now is to manage time. He puts in six to seven hours per day, beyond office hours, on the activities of the council. "My wife is a great help. She has been my moral support," he says.

Committed to the core, Mr. Vaidyanathan is the lone crusader, a David, carrying on a relentless struggle against the Goliath of exploitation and injustice.

Reproduced from: ***Rourkela News***, JAN-MARCH 1989 (In-house magazine of SAIL, Rourkela Steel Plant)

GRAM :
TELEPHONE :

Emblem of
INDIAN OIL

Marketing Division

INDIAN OIL CORPORATION LIMITED
54, Forest Park Road,
Bhubaneswar-751009

In reply please
refer to:
BGM/37
Dt.7.6.85

To
Indane Gas Consumers,
C/o D/609, Sector-8
Rourkela-9

Kind attention: Shri B.Vaidyanathan.

Dear Sirs,

Sub: Home delivery of Indane Refills.

We thankfully acknoludge receipt of your representation dated 29.4.'85.

We are extremely sorry that you are facing very great inconvenience at the stoppage of Home delivery of Indane Gas Refill cylinders by our distributor, M/s Jai Jawan Gas Agency, Rourkela.

We have already taken up the matter very strongly with our distributor and have severely warned them not to take any unilateral decision of stopping home delivery of gas cylinders to our valued customers.

Our Assistant Manager (Sales), Shri B.Mukherjee, posted at Rourkela has been advised to watch the performance of the distributors and ensure that Home delivery is strictly restored. You may kindly contact Shri B. Mukherjee at C-10, Sector-6, Rourkela or on telephone 6075 or 3685 for further assistance.

We assure you that there will be positive improvement in the situation very shortly.

Thanking you and assuring you of our best attention at all times.

Yours faithfully,
for INDIAN OIL

Sd/-
(V.V. Jogiah)
For Divisional Manager

vvj/md.

//Regd.Office 254-C, Dr Annie Besant Road, Prabhadevi
Bombay-400 025(India)
Regional Office: Shakespeare Sarani, CALCUTTA-750071 //

/True copy/

The above letter was received from the Divisional Manager, IOC, Bhubaneswar. This is for information and necessary action from all concerned.

13/06/1985

(B Vaidyanathan)
D/609, Sector-8
Rourkela-9

This book is

dedicated to the fond memories of my father,

Mr. *D.V. Balasubramaniam,*

Who was always with me and encouraged my efforts in every possible way. He was a major donor to the Council and a very valuable well-wisher. Even the draft of this memoir was supposed to be checked by him, but unfortunately he left us abruptly;

&

To the inspiring, courageous & daring memories of my mother,
Mrs. *B. Swarnam,*

whose generosity and hospitality has few parallels.

— B. Vaidyanathan

JUSTICE D.P. WADHWA
Former Judge, Supreme Court of India

President
National Consumer Disputes
Redressal Commission

5th Floor 'A' Wing
Janpath Bhawan, Janpath
New Delhi-110001

Telephone : (+91) (+11) 3327666
Facsimile : (+91) (+11) 3712456

Website : http://consumercom.nic.in

27th October, 2003

Dear Mr. Vaidyanathan,

    I am writing this letter with mixed feelings. Today I have relinquished the charge of the office of the President National Consumer Disputes Redressal Commission (NCDRC) which charge I held for 2-1/2 years.

    I look back with satisfaction the period which I spent in the NCDRC. We have progressed a great deal and were able to cut into past arrears and also able to cope up with daily filing. In State Commissions also working considerably improved in spite of various handicaps. However, that could not be said of every District Forum in the country. Unfortunately, Consumer Forums are fast slipping into the mire of civil courts. This trend has to be checked. But then there is also apathy of State Government and lack of infrastructure. In many District Forums there are few cases and one reasons would be that spread of consumer awareness is quite slow.

    I need not recount the steps taken to improve the working of Consumer Forums all over the country. I wish, however, to tell you that I got complete satisfaction during my tenure in the NCDRC. What I have achieved is all because of your active support and good wishes.

    Consumer Protection Act, 1986 is a unique legislation. The Act saw the light of the day all because of NGOs like you. We must fulfil the objectives with which the Act was passed. A hapless consumer is a victim of red-tapism and corruption. Let him not suffer on account of delayed justice.

    I wish Hon'ble Mr. Justice M.B. Shah success in his new assignment as President, NCDRC.

    With warm regards,

Sincerely,

(D.P. Wadhwa)

Mr. B. Vaidyanathan,
Secretary,
Consumer Protection Council (CPC),
C-66, Sector-2,
Rourkela- 769 006.

Contents

Preface .... *xiii*
Acknowledgements .... *xvii*

Chapter – I
    Birth of the Consumer Protection Council 1

Chapter – II
    Consumer Protection Act 5

Chapter – III
    Advocacy, Consumer Courts and Class Action 9

Chapter – IV
    LPG Under-Weighment Case Exposes the Fallibility of the
    Supreme Court 31

Chapter – V
    Funding – a Perennial Problem 37

Chapter – VI
    Way Forward 41

Annexures
    A. Consumer Dispute Cases Pursued from 1989 – 2014 51
    B. Letter to the Chief Justice of India 63
    C. A letter to the Prime Minister 81
    D. Arnab, et al! There are many more vital things other than
       Sushma bashing! Jago Grahak Jago!! 89

Preface

Looking back – 60 years of my life and having been exposed to public life for almost half of that, I thought it may be worth to share that experience, in my own way. This experience of mine may not necessarily be unique, but the inferences I have derived need some thoughtful consideration.

Every one of us wants India to be a greatly respected and admired country among the comity of nations. We wish it to be a super power, wherein its people enjoy the best standards of living, and that it is not taken for granted even by China or the US, leave alone much smaller nations. The urge for seeking self-respect and justice is inborn in many of us. But are we, as a society and nation comprising individuals, whether it be in administration, judiciary, politics, press or even just as citizens doing the right things which will eventually lead us in that direction?

Everyone is yearning for a change... For a better quality of life.. For a clean and pollution free environment, as in the western countries.. For a society where systems work and it is impersonal.. For a marketplace where a consumer's rights are honoured.. For a society, where there is no corruption.. For a society where crime is put down without any bias.. For a society where individual rights are protected.. For a society where equality is ensured as a rule and not as an exception.. For a society where there is equal opportunity to perform or perish.

If one has to reduce his weight, he has to burn more calories than he is consuming. That burning happens through physical activities. This we all know very well. But when it comes to our behaviour as a member of the society, which ultimately has the potential to lift or destroy the nation, many are either indifferent or irresponsible as to not to appreciate their contribution (positive or negative) to the society at large.

Before I embark upon my venture to share what all I feel worthy of being shared, during my involvement in the consumer movement, which had varied exposures which one can visualise, some personal details which should be of interest are:

- *Born on 30th July 1957, at Chennai, in a family of agriculturists of Ponneri taluk, near Chennai.*

- *Did my Chemical Engineering (1974-79), from Coimbatore Institute of Technology, affiliated to the University of Madras.*

- *After a brief stint in Addison Paints & Chemicals, Chennai, as Plant Chemist Trainee, joined Steel Authority of India Ltd., Rourkela Steel Plant, Rourkela, as Graduate Engineer Trainee, in April 1980. Served there till March 2008, in different capacities as Shift-in-charge to Site-in-charge (AGM), in its Coal Chemicals Unit. My professional employment concluded as COO, of Terra Firma Biotechnologies Ltd., Bengaluru.*

During the course of employment at SAIL, passed Graduateship Examination in Industrial Engineering, Mumbai, in 1984. Subsequently obtained the PG Diploma in Management, of the All India Management Association (AIMA), New Delhi, in 1988. I owe both these qualifications to SAIL, as the incentives awarded therein motivated many of us to go for such qualifications. Similarly, got formal training in Value Engineering, both Module-I and Module-II, under distinguished faculties. That also paved the way for being an in-house faculty for creativity and Value Engineering, until I left the Steel Plant.

Though, I might have had varied experience in my professional life as well as the General Secretary of the Rourkela Steel Plant Executives' Association, this narration is limited to my exposure and experiences in the consumer movement, lasting for more than 31 years, as on date.

Anyone can become a consumer activist, as everyone is engaging himself in the purchase of goods or hiring of services. You do get wronged many a times. Many of us even fight to set right the things. I still recall my experience while I was in my college, at Coimbatore. I had purchased a mechanical alarm time piece from a popular Supermarket. After a few days, I found that it was not functioning properly. I went there to get it attended. They repaired it, but it failed again. After a couple of visits, I requested them to replace the piece. After some arguments, finally the piece was replaced. My roommate Athmasanthi, who was witness to that incident, often used to tease me among friends, as to how I made the life of the salesgirls miserable. I realized, I thought and reacted differently. My inner sense told me it was my father's money and I needed to value it, which led to my other actions. The instinct for seeking fairness and justice must be there in many of us. Some of us shed it off as not worth fighting for while some take that as an opportunity to highlight issues and seek justice. I belong to the latter. In 1985, I stumbled upon the LPG refill supply problem (more about that in the first chapter) and resolved it. That made me realize I could play a bigger role for the larger good. Thus in 1985 a voluntary consumer organisation, Consumer Protection Council, Rourkela was born.

My 31 years of contribution to the Consumer movement were wrought with many challenges and were made possible by a very understanding and accommodative family, comprising of my caring wife Indira and loving daughters, Surya and Aiswarya.

Last but not the least, this venture would not have been possible, but for the sponsorship of my affectionate son-in-law Arun.

8th March 2017
Chennai-61. *B. Vaidyanathan*

Acknowledgements

Though one's individual character, initiatives, abilities and commitment could enable him to do a particular social activity, its reach and success depends on many factors. A major factor is the set of individuals who believed in those common goals and were willing to involve themselves in such an initiative, much more than an ordinary participant or beneficiary and were willing to commit their time, energy and goodwill for such common goals. Though, there can be many who helped me in my journey as a consumer activist, I will be failing in my duty if I fail to acknowledge some outstanding contributors.

I wish to record here the deep appreciation for our Office Assistant cum typist cum volunteer, Mr. T.C.B.Pillai, who was with us for about 15 years of my 23 years association with the Council, at Rourkela. He was a great asset to the Council, till he left Rourkela, for his hometown in Kerala.

I had a committed admirer and volunteer in Mr. B.Panda, from Kolkata, who was always with the Council and its activities, ready to executive any exercise handed over to him, with sincerity and seriousness of a manager. He, on his own could mobilise a set of volunteers to do a particular job. He was a major contributor in our membership drives.

We had another man of action from Kolkata, but with few words, in Mr. B.Mustafi. He was with us, right since inception of the Council, a volunteer par excellence.

Our Council's President for well over 10 years, Mr. V.L.Rao, belonging to Andhra Pradesh, though senior to me in age and position, never had any reservation to participate in the Council's initiatives and made substantial contribution, without any prompting.

Mr. A.P.Biswal, belonging to the Odisha's vernacular press, made very important contribution in almost all the activities that we had taken up, including the establishment of our Consumer Information Centre.

My friend and well-wisher Mr. V.Balasubramanian, though not directly associated as a volunteer, did come to our rescue, as and when needed.

I personally miss my friend Late B.Gopal, who abruptly passed away in 1998. His zeal and commitment had few parallels.

All my efforts at the Supreme Court were made possible by Late Badridas Sharma, of Jodhpur, Rajasthan, an Advocate at the Supreme Court. Seldom have you come across such a genuine and humble person who stood apart in serving the people with the human touch. But for his magnanimous support to allow me to freely use his office in the Lawyers' Chamber, in the hallowed precincts of the Supreme Court, I could not have pursued any of my cases in the apex Court of law.

I am indeed thankful to my daughter Surya, who volunteered to provide me the much needed editing assistance, in spite of her busy schedule stretched between a demanding toddler and managerial responsibilities in office, at Seattle, US.

B. Vaidyanathan

Chapter – 1

Birth of the Consumer Protection Council

Every calamity throws up challenges and opportunities. If one can seize those opportunities, there is a huge scope for betterment and growth. It was in October 1984, that the then Prime Minister of India, Smt. Indira Gandhi was assassinated by her own security guards. As many of you will recall, that incident resulted in widespread violence against the Sikhs across the country, especially in the northern parts of the country.

In Rourkela also some stray incidents of violence took place against that community due to the grief and dissent among the population. The local *Indane* gas distributor, M/s Jai Jawan Gas Service happened to be owned by a Sikh. His shop was also partially damaged during that unrest. On the pretext of getting his shop repaired and the insurance claim settled, he suspended cooking gas booking from that shop, suspended home delivery and asked customers to visit his godown (warehouse), located at a place outside the Steel City and carry the gas refills (weighing around 30 kgs) themselves. Since the said *Indane* distributor had a good reputation of providing prompt and efficient service, the customers initially willingly obliged him. But there was no indication of an end to this self-service, even after a couple of months. People started grumbling, but no one was willing to take appropriate action to highlight that problem to the concerned authorities. That continued for 4 months. In Jan. 1985, since the resentment was growing, some of the customers started representing the problem to the Indian Oil Corporation (IOC), in an anonymous manner, i.e. without providing their identity, consumer number or full address. It is pertinent to note here that many of those people who had represented that problem of the dealer, had cautiously avoided providing their personal details, thereby giving a room for IOC to interpret it as a bogus complaint. As a result, the problem was not resolved.

Though we have officials designated to handle escalations in such situations, for e.g. in this case, the Assistant Manager (LPG), stationed at Rourkela, most of them are, content to remain as a wilful spectator, until they are forced to act. The obvious reason being their close association with the distributor and the relationship that develops between them, resulting in a soft corner; and further the unpleasant act to curb their inappropriate practice is by and large overlooked as there is no deterrent to force them into such action, which at times could be even unsafe. That is more so, in remoter areas.

It was in March 1985 that I came to know about the harassment by the *Indane* distributor. I had gone to book for a gas refill, as my wife was to return back to Rourkela, along with our first baby daughter. The distributor refused to make the booking and informed me that they had the clearance from the concerned authorities for the practice (Cash and Carry) adopted by them to force the consumers to lift the refill cylinder from their godown. I politely told him that as the dealer it is his job to service the customers and not otherwise. But he was adamant and challenged me to do whatever I wanted. Thereafter I initiated a letter to the concerned authorities including the then Union Minister, about the plight of the *Indane* consumers of Rourkela, stating my address, Consumer Number, etc. To add weight to this complaint, I made an effort to mobilise all the affected individuals across the Steel Township, with a clear instruction that those interested in joining the campaign should record their name, signature, consumer number and address. Since by that time many were already fed up with this harassment, and since someone was willing to take the lead and get identified, within a span of a week, more than 300 individuals had signed the petition. That petition was sent to the concerned authorities of the government and IOC.

To the pleasant surprise of everyone, within a week, I received a communication from IOC, regretting for whatever had happened and also assuring that "Home Delivery" would be restored forthwith and the dealer's shop, which was hitherto located outside the Township, would be shifted to a central place, in the township.

After the "Home Delivery" of cooking gas got restored, the residents of the township really started feeling that things were indeed moving, with systematic efforts. It was during that period, that I made efforts through informal and unorganised communication channels about the relevance and need for an organised effort to address various consumer issues affecting them, in day to day life.

I initiated a meeting of like-minded individuals, at Rourkela Club, on Sunday, 8th September 1985, and extended an open invitation for all those interested to join, discuss and explore options to form a voluntary organisation for safeguarding their interests as consumers. Though I was young and had very less exposure to Rourkela, around 25 residents came for the Meeting and unanimously supported the idea of starting the voluntary organisation to be known as Consumer Protection Council, Rourkela. I was selected as its Secretary, with the mandate to enrol more members and complete the Registration formalities. It was decided to collect an Annual Subscription of Rs. 2/- per member. (I continued to be the Secretary, till I left Rourkela, in 2008.)

Thus Consumer Protection Council, Rourkela, was formed to take care of various issues affecting the consumers, more than a year before the versatile and landmark Consumer Protection Act came into being, in December 1986.

To give the much needed initial thrust to our endeavour, I approached the then GM(Works) of the Roukela Steel Plant, Late Subrata Ray, to join our Council and be its President. After some questioning he agreed to be the President. Rest is history, as they say. Because of his presence, the Council got the fillip it needed and hundreds joined in no time. That beginning indeed ensured the association of several top executives of the Steel fraternity, like Mr. Brijlal Kshatriya, Mr. A.K.Fotedar and Mr. R.C.Mohanty, with the Council, for quite some time.

Several initiatives were taken right from inception for resolving issues affecting the public or the individuals at large, and even before formal registration of the Council had been completed. From the beginning we took the appropriate initiatives for creating consumer awareness, education and protection. We organised regular interaction with representatives of state administration, like the Additional District Magistrate, Superintendent of Police, income tax authorities like the Asst. Commissioner of Income Tax and many others. Our endeavour was always to educate the consumer, so that he/she can independently safeguard his/her interests. Thus, after the registration of the Council, in 1987, I initiated steps for publishing Council's monthly newsletter, which was circulated among our members and the general public. In January 1989, our registered English monthly newspaper, *Advantage Consumer* was first published and has been till date.

The Council had always tried to rise to the needs of the consumers, especially at Rourkela, whether it be Omfed milk supply, public distribution – Ration shops, non-refunding of booking advance by LML, etc. Literally any problem being faced by the residents was immediately referred to us; that was the faith we could create within a short time. Thus, going to the consumer courts, naturally became the next logical step in our journey, when our efforts in ADR (Alternate Disputes Resolution) failed.

I may not appear to be modest, when I say that I had always been savvy to technological developments around me. But the fact, though I might be a bit rustic when I am found lying on the floor, in an unreserved railway compartment, when a need arises, I always had an eye for adopting to the latest technological developments or to leverage them for economy and work simplification. Thus, in 1995 itself we started our desk top publishing of our monthly Advantage Consumer. In the year 2000, after we established the Consumer Information Centre and our captive Library, we launched our website *www.advantageconsumer.com*.

Through this website, till date, I have been answering the queries of the consumers, from across the country, and even other parts of the world, *free of cost*. Though I had to leave Rourkela in April 2008 for personal reasons, I continue to be associated with this voluntary consumer organisation, as per need and as desired by our Council collective, as its Chief Mentor.

Chapter – II

Consumer Protection Act

Many developed countries, even by the middle of the 20th century had established a comprehensive mechanism and legal framework for dealing with the protection of consumer rights, thereby striking a balance between a flourishing market economy and consumers' interests. But in underdeveloped countries and developing nations, such legal frameworks and mechanisms were conspicuous by their absence. So, in 1985, the United Nations framed the guidelines for consumer protection, and wanted the member nations to adopt it for the benefit of their citizens, who were being taken for a ride by some of the unscrupulous traders and businesses.

Though India had several legislations for safeguarding the consumer interests, even before 1985, like the Prevention of Food & Adulteration Act, Standards of Weights and Measures Act, and so on, those were aimed at punishing the culprit for non-adherence to standards, like the milk vendor or the trader. The procedures were cumbersome and time consuming, giving wider scope for the Inspectors to make hay, while delivering hardly any compensation to the aggrieved nor any effective mechanism for redressal of his grievance. In this context, the UN guidelines of 1985 prompted the Government of India, to devise a legislation for safeguarding the consumer interests, whether while purchasing goods or availing services.

The landmark Consumer Protection Act, enacted in 1986, on the broad guidelines of the UN, provides for a 3-tier quasi-judicial machinery, comprising of: (a) District Consumer Disputes Redressal Forum, in short, the District Forum, at the district level; (b) State Consumer Disputes Redressal Commission, in short, the State Commission, at the State level; and (c) the National Consumer Disputes Redressal Commission, in short, the National Commission, at the apex national level. All these three levels of bodies are collectively referred to as the consumer courts. The National Commission's verdict can be challenged only in the Supreme Court. These grievance redressal machineries are supposed to function without the frills of a civil court, wherein an affected consumer can seek redress in terms of replacement and/or compensation, in a time bound manner. In cases where no laboratory analysis is required to be undertaken to confirm the consumer's allegation, the Consumer Courts are supposed to pronounce their order, within 90 days. In such other cases, where laboratory analysis is required to confirm the consumer's allegations, a maximum time limit of 180 days, has been prescribed.

This Act, which has envisaged a quasi-judicial approach in redressing the grievances, is a landmark deviation from the earlier enactments which is supposed to enable even the lay consumers with some level of drafting abilities to approach these quasi-judicial bodies in person, without having the need to approach or avail the services of a professionally qualified lawyer. As a matter of principle and practice, these consumer courts are to be presided by legally qualified judicial officials and individuals of standing from non-legal backgrounds, and hence the term quasi-judicial body. It is another point that such a progressive piece of legislation has not been able to deliver commensurate results due to public apathy, legal hyper technicalities being adopted by the presiding members of the consumer courts and even the Supreme Court. It makes one sad that a big democracy like ours should suffer because of such ineptitude of the judiciary. More about this in the chapter on "Fallibility of the Supreme Court".

This Act has been enacted to safeguard the 6 Consumer Rights, which have been stated in this Act. These Rights include: (1) The Right to be informed about the quality and quantity of goods or services; (2) The Right to be protected against the goods and services, which can cause injury; (3) The Right to be heard in all appropriate fora; (4) The Right to Redressal of grievances; (5) The Right to multiple choice of goods; and (6) The Right to consumer education. Similarly, to promote and protect the Rights of the Consumers, the Act envisages establishing of consultative bodies such as the State Consumer Protection Councils, at the level of States and the Central Consumer Protection Council, at the national level, to meet and deliberate periodically about the problems in the implementation of the Act, the problems and the shortcomings faced in protecting the Rights of the Consumers, as envisaged in the Consumer Protection Act.

The Central Consumer Protection Council is supposed to be headed by the Minister In-charge of Consumer Affairs of the Union government and is supposed to have members representing various interest groups like the voluntary consumer organisations (VCOs), trade and industry, state governments, central government and its agencies, etc. This body which was supposed to meet thrice in a year, was subsequently amended to meet at least once in a year. Such a good progress achieved, within 7 years of enactment of the Act(?)

While any amendment to the Consumer Protection Act, as with any other law requires the sanction of the Parliament, by smart amendments to the Rules framed under the Act, the political class can in effect manipulate the Act to suit their convenience. The case in point is the effective castration of the Central Consumer Protection Council, in 2006. For amendment to the Consumer Protection Rules, wherein the enabling provisions of the Act have been laid down, with the concurrence of the then Union Minister (Mr. Sharad Pawar – this year's *Padma Vibhushan* nominee), without much publicity and parliamentary intervention, a sound and effective mechanism like the Central Consumer Protection Council (CCPC) was made ineffective, practically to disenfranchise the vociferous consumer groups, which have been making cohesive and joint efforts to highlight consumer issues of substance, at the national level. **Because of the amendments brought about in the Consumer Protection Rules, in 2006, the size of the Central Council was drastically reduced from about 160+ to about 35, an 80% reduction.** As a result of this reduction, much lesser members (activists) get represented in this body. While today, we have 36 states and union territories, only representatives of 5 consumer groups get represented in this body, for a period of 3 years. Which means, consumer groups of every state will get an opportunity to be represented only once in 21 years, assuming that there is no repetition of the members so nominated, i.e., not re-nominated, for a period of 21 years. *Hold on!!*

The venomous amendment further permits only representatives of such voluntary consumer organisations which are members of Consumers International, to be nominated to the CCPC. What a ridiculous amendment? Instead of strengthening the consumer organisations, it is a clear intent to weaken them. Why so? Because, consumer organisations which are struggling to make both ends meet, are being compelled to take a membership of an international organisation, whose membership charges, running into hundreds of dollars, are simply beyond the realm of affordability for overwhelming majority of the consumer groups. But without the CI membership, their representatives will not be considered for the nomination. The fact is that only a handful of consumer organisations enjoy this costly membership, out of thousands which are existing today. This is true for the state government representatives as well. This does not augur well for the consumers as a whole. May be, the thinking is that the central government and its staff are good enough to take care of the consumers and it might be better to reduce the role of the civil society in such an endeavour. It is no surprise that the quasi-judicial bodies have not been performing as mandated by the Act. The apathy of state governments, as well as that of the centre for ensuring the enforcement of the Act has gone to such indifferent levels that existence of such a progressive legislation is becoming more and more irrelevant.

Chapter – III

Advocacy, Consumer Courts and Class Action

As an individual, I have always questioned the *status quo* and had a bent of mind for rational thinking, logical approach and earned a reputation of being a maverick. That is why, probably, though not being legally qualified, I had ventured to do things in a manner which could be termed as even path-breaking. For example, to attract public attention, and to convey the message to the consumers, commercial establishments have the habit of putting up hoardings and signboards. But, in 1988-89 itself, we in the Council had put up a signboard, of size 5 M X 3 M, highlighting the salient features of the Standards of Weights and Measures Act, asking the public to read the label (MRP/Expiry Date), in a prominent location, in front of the *Ispat Market* (the Central Market of the Steel Township). Similarly, in 1990, we had also erected another hoarding of size 8 M x 3 M, highlighting the harmful effects of junk food, as was publicised by the International Organisation of Consumers Union (presently known as Consumers International). To our credit, we had the first sanction, from Ministry of Food, Civil Supplies & Consumer Affairs, Government of India, in 1991, for putting up such a hoarding, to educate the consumers.

Success through Advocacy

Separate District Forum for Rourkela

Though Consumer Courts (District Fora and the State Commission) were established in Odisha, in 1989, the District Forum for Sundergarh district, in which Rourkela is situated, was located at the district headquarters, Sundergarh, 100 KM away from Rourkela. There was a real problem for filing and pursuing consumer dispute cases in the District Forum relating to Rourkela. Since, right from the beginning the Council was functioning on a very tight budget and since I was keen to develop the Council on an independent platform, so that it is capable of handling the cases on its own, each date in a case entailed travelling to Sundergarh, and thus wastage of one full day. That problem was naturally faced by anyone who wanted to pursue his consumer dispute case in the District Forum. A big disincentive for filing case in the consumer court was thus in-built in the system. Consumer Dispute cases worthy of even less than Rs. 1,000/- needed to be filed and pursued in this cumbersome and costly manner. Interestingly, Rourkela being commercially vibrant due to the presence of the Steel Plant and many ancillary industries, enjoyed the status of being the highest contributor of Consumer Dispute Cases, in the District Forum (>90%). The irony made us take up this issue with the state government, to avoid the colossal loss to the nation, in terms of the man hours lost in transit, precious fuel consumed in such avoidable visits and obvious monetary loss to those involved in the cases. Highlighting these problems faced by the consumers of Rourkela, we represented the matter to the Government of Orissa. The issue was not addressed.

The Central Consumer Protection Council (CCPC), the apex consultative body, with representatives from consumer groups from all the states and union territories, state government officials and the respective Ministers for Food & Civil Supplies, Central agencies, National Commission and headed by the Union Minister for Food, Civil Supplies and Consumer Affairs, used to have a big appeal in those days. The meetings were invariably held in the Parliament House Annexe, giving it a special status, befitting the importance "Consumer Protection" was enjoying those days. To illustrate the importance further, I would like to recall that the then Prime Minister Sri P.V.Narasimha Rao, attended one of the Meetings, in 1992, to assure that the government will do everything to support the cause of the consumers. Because those Meetings attracted so much importance and attention, the proceedings were invariably reported in the government owned *Doordarshan*, the dominant TV channel in those days. I had represented the Council, in the Central Consumer Protection Council, consistently from 1989. I had the privilege to highlight the unique problems of the residents of Rourkela, at Sundergarh. That immediately attracted wide attention among the members of the CCPC and the Minister of Food & Civil Supplies, Odisha, Late Bhagabat Behera, assured that the government would look into the problem. As per our wishes, within a year with the consent of the then Chief Minister, Late

Biju Patnaik, a separate District Forum was sanctioned for Rourkela, designated as Sundergarh-II. That success, something great, had happened because of the consultative mechanism of CCPC, envisaged in the Consumer Protection Act, and has benefitted entire Rourkela and peripheral areas. Incidentally, Sundergarh continues to be one of the few districts in the country, wherein two District Forums are functioning, to cater to the aggrieved consumers.

Advocacy involves systematically pursuing the issue of interest in the appropriate forum, whether it be in the consultative bodies, government agencies or even with the government or their representatives, so as to resolve the issue. As an activist or as a representative of a voluntary organisation, one should remember the limitations and the role which you are expected to play because success does not come so easily in a system whose constituents at times have conflicting interests. For example, in 1993 or so, in the wake of economic liberalisation, Government of India, in order to give a boost to industrial production and growth, announced Excise Duty concessions on a gamut of industrial products consumed by the households. Though concessions were announced, good many of the manufacturers did not pass on the benefit to the common man. Since I had collated all the details, both from the market and excise duty manuals, I personally took up the issue with the then Union Minister, Mr. A.K.Antony, who was the Chairman of the CCPC, and handed him the details. Sri Antony did try to pursue the issue for the benefit of the people, but unfortunately Dr. Manmohan Singh, who was the then Finance Minister, took the stand that the concession had been extended for ensuring the economic growth of the industry. However illogical it may be, the consumer groups could hardly do anything about that. The point is advocacy campaigns need not necessarily result in success and voluntary groups ought to realise that and proceed.

"*Doordarshan*" TV transmitter relocated

But, we had our share of success on several occasions. One such was the relocation of the *Doordarshan* TV transmitter on the elevated and centrally located Durgapur Hills. During the 80s, when the TV viewers depended solely on *Doordarshan* and antenna for receiving the TV signals, the picture reception used to be very poor in the Steel Township, due to the transmitter being on the plains and Rourkela being situated amidst hilly areas. I had written about this to Director (Engineering), in *Mandi House*, Headquarters of *Doordarshan*. To our pleasant surprise, they promptly informed us that they will shift the TV transmitter to the elevated Durgapur Hills, near the Microwave Tower, which was already existing. During one of my visits to Delhi those days, when I visited *Mandi House*, they shared the details with enthusiasm and were eager to avail my services for getting periodical feedback about the progress at the site, so that the shifting can be expedited. Because of such an encouragement and enthusiasm, I had made it a routine to visit the site on Sundays, at least once in a fortnight or so, when the site did not even have access through a proper motorable road. (Of course, subsequently, after the completion of the project, they had laid a road.) So, it was an adventurous journey, every fortnight or so, to move on a two-wheeler, on a steep slope, when the then Council's Joint Secretary, B.Mustafi, used to accompany me on such visits. Thus, this campaign culminated with the shifting of the TV transmitter, benefitting the entire Rourkela city. But, it is another point that an overwhelming majority are now depending on cable TV.

Our Role in the Electricity Regulatory Commission

My foray into the Electricity Regulatory Commission is worth sharing. Electricity Reforms had become necessary due to the systemic inefficiencies and non-objective fixing of tariff resorted to by the political class, thereby literally making the electricity sector unhealthy and sick. After the economic liberalisation policies that were introduced in the 90s, to ensure building up a robust infrastructure capable of supporting and sustaining industrial growth, for bringing in efficiency and objectivity, participation of private companies and their capital became essential and the reforms in the electricity sector became inevitable.

I had the privilege of being nominated to the Commission Advisory Committee (CAC) of the Orissa Electricity Regulatory Commission (OERC), ever since it started functioning in 1996 or so, and was a member till I left Orissa in 2008. The regulatory mechanism which has unquestionably brought about objectivity in assessing the tariff is determined through meticulous evaluation of the demands of the generating (GENCOs), transmitting (TRANSCOs) and distributing (DISTCOs) entities (Companies). Having experienced the functioning of the Commission Advisory Committee of the Electricity Regulatory Commission, which is constituted with representatives of the major industrial consumers, like the Railways, domestic consumers and consumer groups, and domain experts, systematically goes through the various documents, which are required to be submitted to the Commission, by the said Companies. The Regulatory Commission, which is backed up by a well-staffed office, objectively assesses the revenue requirement, in consultation with the CAC and after open public hearing, the tariff is finally ascertained. Thanks to these Regulatory mechanisms, one of the major ills of the electricity sector, namely, the Transmission & Distribution Losses (T&D Losses), which is the root cause of the institutionalised inefficiencies and theft got highlighted and addressed by everyone, including the honest consumer. The Regulatory mechanism also played an important role for ensuring quality of electricity as well as billing and service, especially in Orissa, wherein improper Billing and Metering were quite rampant. The only major shortcoming in the system, as was experienced by me, was the politics associated with the fixing of tariff and the lack of objective steps that are taken by the state government to minimise the T&D losses. These two, obviously prevent right projection of the benefits of the Regulatory exercise among the public.

It is in this background one has to view the fictitious allegations of anti-corruption crusader like Mr. Arvind Kejriwal that the DERC (Delhi Electricity Regulatory Commission) was siphoning out huge money in favour of Reliance and Tata Power Companies. When such allegations were aired, I used to wonder as to how responsible people can make such wild allegations, without even understanding the Regulatory mechanism. As expected by me, Kejriwal could never prove his allegations, but rather preferred to act like a seasoned politician, to dish out huge concession to the electricity consumers of Delhi. The point is regulatory mechanism is a positive development to have taken place in this country. 50 years of mismanagement cannot be rectified overnight and the best interests of the consumers are served only when everyone takes part and addresses the shortcomings with objectivity. Naturally, that requires understanding the price fixing mechanism and doing good amount of home work to pin point the shortcomings in the proposal. Thus advocacy involves doing good amount of homework, with objectivity.

Council and ADR

As we embarked on our advocacy campaign, for achieving the desired goals, on issues which are by and large affecting large cross sections of the society, we also devised our own Alternate Dispute Redressal (ADR) mechanism almost since inception of our Council. Individuals were encouraged to lodge their complaints with necessary documentary evidence and to facilitate individuals who were interested to meet in person, I was personally meeting them on Sundays, in the Council's office, during morning hours and on Wednesdays, during evening hours, in our Consumer Information Centre. The complaints so received were referred to the concerned business establishment. Good majority of the complaints (>80%) were getting resolved through such correspondence itself, or in some cases over telephonic contact. But, when disputes were not getting resolved through such methods, depending on the type of dispute, evidences in favour of the consumer and provided the consumer individual is also keen to get it resolved through legal means, we were approaching the consumer court. Because of such methodical screening and diligence exercised in filing the cases, it is to the credit of the Council, that overwhelming majority of the cases had been decided in favour of the Council/consumer litigant and they also received the intended (ordered) monetary and/or other benefits. It may be surprising for many of you to know that all the services including pursuing court cases were totally rendered free of cost. As Secretary and later as Chief Mentor of the Council, I had taken the responsibility to represent the matter, in the Courts. The gist of cases pursued are available in Annexure-A.

Class Action Cases

Non-refunding of Booking Advance by M/s LML

Whether you pursue a case in the consumer court for one individual or a small or a large group or the community at large, as I have experienced, the efforts are not much different in terms of making a draft for filing in the court or going to the court on hearing days. While in respect of individual cases, the concerned individual himself brings, by and large, the requisite details, in case of Class Action Cases (PILs) the onus of collecting the necessary particulars rests with the organisation pursuing the issue. Though, this could be an important issue, apart from this, there are no other major differences. But, the class or public interest petitions have the potential to benefit large cross-sections of the society and a phenomenal visibility to a voluntary organisation, and hence such cases are worth the efforts. Furthermore, since a voluntary organisation is starved of resources of all kinds, to make effective use of whatever is available, it makes sense to file class action petitions affecting a large number of individuals. Thus, ever since the consumer courts started functioning, we began utilising them for redressing the grievances of a class of consumers. *That's how we were probably the first in the entire country, in taking up common complaints of group of individuals, to the consumer courts.* In 1989 itself, our complaint petitions against M/s Lohia Machines Ltd. (LML) and M/s Andhra Pradesh Scooters Ltd. (APSL), for non-refunding of booking advance, were filed in the State Commission, Orissa, Cuttack (CD Case No. 48 and 49 of 1989, respectively), rather, *the first ever case that was filed on behalf of Consumer Protection Council, Rourkela.* Those complaint petitions made up of 87 complainants, in respect of M/s LML and 24 complainants, in respect of M/s APSL, of Orissa, who had complained to the Council.

As a student of engineering I always had the habit of working out the details through application of logic, nothing more. Though a novice at the courts, and an outsider to the legal fraternity, without much exposure or guidance from those who practice law, after going through the Consumer Protection Act, I thought of clubbing all the individual complaints, which were of the same nature against the same opposite party, M/s LML, and that gave the requisite weightage of over Rs. 1 lakh, including the quantified losses, making it possible to approach the State Commission, directly. There was no objection from any quarter, regarding the jurisdictional aspect, and we won the case and the complainant individuals got their refunds along with interest.

Immediately, after the initial victory, and having known that individuals across the country were affected by the same problem of non-refunds, we ventured to take up that issue on the national level. Thanks to our 'Press Release' getting publicised by the newspapers, our initiative attracted around 1,800 complaints from individuals from across the country against M/s LML and M/s APSL, within a week or so. The response was so huge that even the local Post Office had difficulties in delivering the mail, as many of them had responded by Registered Post and the delivery on the last day or two, warranted the Post Man to hire a rickshaw for delivery! (This I vividly remember, as there was an altercation between our office-boy and the postman, for his inability to deliver such huge amount of mails received during that time.) Thereafter, to be able to file the petition, in the National Commission, a mammoth task was undertaken. Many of my friends and well-wishers volunteered and helped us to take out the individual details, such as name, address, date of booking, date of cancellation, partial refund received, if any, and the date of receipt. I had always tried to do a thorough job of the complaint petition, as well as the supporting data, that I had to utilise the Personal Computer (PC), which had arrived by then in Rourkela. At times, the Courts where such petitions are filed hardly appreciate the humongous exercise, could be disappointing indeed. But, habits don't change and till this day I have been adhering to my standards, for my own satisfaction. With the help of dBase software, which was quite popular for handling large data with ease, we could generate voluminous reports running into 100s of pages, detailing the status of each complainant individual and the compensation payable to them, which was filed as Annexure to our Original Petition filed before the National Commission, in 1990 (APSL – Original Petition No. 29 of 1990; LML- Original Petition No. 30 of 1990). As a souvenir of this mammoth case, I am retaining these two voluminous reports with me. These cases gave us some prominence in those days, but one cannot help wondering as to why the public jumped into the bandwagon and booked for a vehicle when many of them neither knew about the vehicle, nor had a need for it. *Unless this mob mentality changes, consumers are likely to be taken for a ride in future also.*

Upkeep of Utkal Kalinga Express

Thereafter, in 1991, we had another important case filed in the National Commission (Original Petition No. 17 of 1991), against the Northern Railways for improper maintenance and upkeep of the toilets in the Utkal Kalinga Express, that ran between Puri, in Orissa and Hazrat Nizamuddin, in New Delhi. That initiative resulted in the introduction of midway cleaning and upkeep of the toilets and the bogies, in all long distance trains in a big way.

Fleecing passengers traveling by Air

We handled another interesting problem in 1993. In cities like Rourkela, where there were no air services, Indian Airlines did not have a Booking Office and in those days, online booking had not been introduced. So the residents of Rourkela, had to avail the offline Travel Agents, who used to arrange the air ticket from their associates in Kolkata, for a charge. This charge was not regulated by the Indian Airlines, resulting in the air passengers acceding to the demands made by the Travel Agent. This was an irritant and since Indian Airlines did not come forward to sort out the issue, we approached the National Commission, as it affected thousands of air passengers across the country. The National Commission did not allow the case, as the Consumer Protection Act that existed at that point in time, did not provide for filing Public Interest Cases and only affected consumers could approach it for seeking relief. The necessary changes got introduced in the Act, later in June that year. Interestingly, after having observed the National Commission having enlarged its jurisdiction on its own in its order for the LML case, to cover all those who had made a booking in the LML case, at the instance of leading advocates of the Supreme Court who had represented that Company, in 1992, the said technical approach was indeed intriguing. After all a court is a court. The fact remains that the defaulting company (LML) was dragged to various courts and District Forums, across the country, by the invested public, making its life miserable. Thus getting a solution at a single point (National Commission), on reasonable terms was to LML's advantage. Incidentally, the necessary amendments to the Consumer Protection Act in sec. 2(1)(b), relating to "complainant", came about in June 1993, a couple of months after our case was dismissed. *An activist needs to be ready to face such ironies.*

The RDA Case

In spite of the Consumer Protection Act, even the state owned undertakings appear to care a damn for the paying consumer. This we had seen in the famous Lucknow Development Authority case and many others. Similar thing happened to the individuals who booked their houses with the Rourkela Development Authority (RDA). The case related to violation of plan and specifications and an inordinate delay in handing over the possession of the houses. As we often come across, in the euphoria and excitement to get quicker resolution of the problem on hand, and due to lack of proper guidance, individuals create more problems for themselves so as to make the entire episode a nightmare of their life. This matter which involved several individuals, with each case worth approximately a couple of lakhs, could have easily been taken up directly through the National Commission, had they all joined together, rather than filing individual cases. *It is my experience and considered view that the apex Commission had always been functioning much better than the lower Commissions or the Fora, and if there is a scope it is always better to go to the apex body, as the time lost is minimal in terms of appeals and reviews and the verdict is binding.* Further it is seen that the systems are better adhered in the apex body and the competence levels are also much higher, for obvious reasons. The only appeal possible is in the Supreme Court.

The State Commission of Orissa, where the individuals had filed their complaint, after elaborate comments about the inefficient functioning of the state undertaking, etc. gave a directive to the RDA, the Opposite Party, to constitute a Committee to ascertain whether the allegations of the individuals were indeed correct and to suggest actions needed for resolving those issues. How can an alleged culprit himself be asked to judge, is a fundamental question which could arise to any sane human being, but the State Commission did not have any hesitation to pronounce such an order. Heeding to the fervent pleas of the concerned individuals and considering that an institution installed to protect the consumers, cannot go overboard and penalise them in such a blatant manner, we entered the fray in 1995, in the appeal stage. Though we did win the case for them, but the enormous delay (National Commission to State Commission to National Commission to Supreme Court and finally National Commission to State Commission, for execution of the order), which occurred due to the initial flaw (of approaching the State Commission, individually) did not help many of the litigants, as they kept moving out of the case and lost any benefit from the litigation. This case for me, amply demonstrates the lessons for the prospective litigants. ***They ought to consider the likely delays which they will have to put up with, in case they are indeed interested to seek justice in a court in this country.*** Further, after having decided to fight, one should be mentally prepared to wait till the end if they are eager to reap the benefits, that too when a voluntary organisation is transparently pursuing their interests. But, as far as the housing issue is concerned, the consumer has the right to seek legal remedy even after obtaining possession of the house, if he is in a position to prove the shortcomings in the construction, in terms of plan and specification violations. But the bandwagon psyche does the trick, I suppose.

NSC-VI issue fraud

Another interesting case which needs to be mentioned, though it was fought for one individual, is the NSC (National Savings Certificate) VI issue case. That case was initiated in 1994, on behalf of the then DIG of Police, Western Range, Orissa. A classic case that shows how even an educated individual can be duped by the government's own Postal Department. As per the NSC document, on maturity, he was supposed to be paid at a particular rate of interest along with the principal. The interest rates for the six year deposits in the National Savings Certificate (NSC VI issue) were revised downward since 1-4-87 and accordingly the depositor was to receive Rs. 114/-

less than the maturity amount mentioned on the Certificate, per thousand, at the time of maturity. The Government had made public this change through Gazette Notifications. But at the same time through the said notifications instructed that the NSC VI issue Certificates with revised interest rates should bear a statement written or affixed by rubber stamp that "Maturity value revised. See notification GSR No. 364(E), dated 1-4-87". Mr. G.C.Nanda, the affected individual, who was not aware of the changed interest rates purchased Certificates worth Rs. 20,000, between March to July 1988. None of the Certificates bore the "prescribed" statement that the "maturity value had been revised", as required by the notifications. At the time of maturity he received lesser money than what was printed on the Certificates. The matter was referred to the Council and the Council went up to the Hon'ble National Commission. Sadly all the three quasi-judicial bodies decided that it was a *clerical error* on the part of the issuing official and that there was no deficiency in service. *Many times, especially when the government or its agencies are involved, it is observed that the courts tend to apply a logic that "Head, the Opposite Party wins and Tail, the consumer loses".* If the gazette notification is indeed so sacrosanct, why did the Postal Authorities failed to implement it, while issuing the Certificates, not once, but on multiple occasions, between March to July, as was pointed out in the case? By a simple excuse that it was clerical error, should the courts be a party to such wanton dereliction of duty, amounting to fraud? Further, it is pertinent to note that since the deposits fell during that period, NSC interests were enhanced once again from 01.04.1989.

Bokaro-Alleppey Express and Management of traffic

The next case in my narration relates to Bokaro-Alleppey Express train, which was the only link till the 90s, serving the travelling public of the steel cities of Bokaro, Ranchi, Tatanagar, Rourkela, of the eastern parts of the country and the southern states of Andhra Pradesh, Tamilnadu and Kerala. That train was running as the Tatanagar Express, in the 60s, linking Tatanagar and Chennai, was pretty old and an important direct train to the steel cities, from the south. Such a long distance train was not being given due care and was one of the most neglected trains one can imagine. One of its specialities was the arrival departure timings, which used to be very early morning, 3 AM or so, while coming from Rourkela and leaving Chennai, late in the night, around 11 PM or so. Till the 90s, the only consolation we had was that it was at least a direct train departing and arriving at Chennai Central Station. Suddenly, in July 1994, this train was handpicked and given a special treatment, and it was diverted via Perambur, in the western corridor of Chennai, subjecting the rail passengers of this train to enormous hardship, as the Perambur sub-urban station is nowhere near the facilities provided at the Chennai Central. As a matter of fact, the said Railway station did not even have a covered platform. This special treatment to a train, which was passing through Chennai at odd hours was taken up on behalf of the Council and we approached the National Commission, in 1995 (Original Petition No. 8 of 1995). Southern Railway explained that due to congestion at the Chennai Central and railway platform work, to accommodate longer length passenger trains, they had diverted the train via Perambur. They were also planning to divert more trains via Perambur and would develop all the facilities, they submitted. The National Commission observed that the Railways can divert trains for management of traffic and management of traffic was not a service which was being rendered for a consideration. Hence, did not provide any relief. But, subsequent to the National Commission's decision, the train was restored to its previous route, via Chennai Central, benefitting thousands of rail passengers.

Remember that nothing (*Indane*) is indispensable

We had another case, which resulted in the suspension of '*Indane*' LPG dealership of the Rourkela Steel Township, and in the appointment of a new dealer, benefitting the residents of the Township. In 1997, the local 'Indane' dealer stopped taking bookings and made it mandatory for the residents to pick up their refill from the dealer's godown or shop. We were compelled to approach the State Commission, Orissa (CD case No. 13 of 1997) after the IOC authorities failed to interfere in an effective manner. Due to our initiative and with the directions of the State Commission, the said dealership was suspended and a new dealer was appointed. All this, took about 10 months or so. I will not be able to forget this case for a couple of reasons. One is that the dealership was with our own Hindustan Steel Workers Credit Cooperative Society (HSWCCS), because of which I had come under some pressure, from our own senior colleagues (of the Steel Plant); of course, appreciating our objective work and the problems faced by the housewives, and knowing my single minded approach, they did not venture to influence me beyond a point. The second one is more personal. My household went without cooking gas for about 6 months, as I was particular on doing the right thing and insisted on the home delivery of the LPG refill. Of course, some of my friends did offer to bring the refill on my behalf or supply their spare refill. I believe that nothing is indispensable. So, why not learn to live with whatever is at your disposal. (After all, being in the Steel Township, we had access to quality electricity and kerosene.) *It is ultimately your attitude which can bring you peace and happiness.* Having understood me and appreciating the logic in my approach, my wife and children fully cooperated and managed those 6 months or so well. Only thing, we went without *'dosa's* during that period. *The moral is that if as a consumer you want to assert your right, be willing to make some small sacrifices and remember that nothing is indispensable.*

Unfair Trade Practice adopted by Railways

We took up another blatant case of "deficient service", by the Indian Railways, which was not appropriately considered either by the National Commission (OP No. 292 of 1996) or the Supreme Court (Civil Appeal No. 48 of 1999). The only solace is that though no favourable pronouncement could be obtained in those two courts, consumer interests were safeguarded because of our dogged approach to achieve the results. The case relates to Ispat Express, run by the South Eastern Railway. This day time train running between Howrah, in Kolkata and Sambalpur, in Odisha, was catering to the travellers of Kharagpur, in West Bengal, Tatanagar, in Jharkhand, Rourkela and Sambalpur, in Odisha. Since the distance between Howrah and most of the cities up to Rourkela, could be covered within a span of 6 hours or so, many preferred it, as it was the only day time Express train. That train had an AC Chair Car, which was always in demand, because of hot summers. For reasons which are not clear, the South Eastern Railway withdrew the AC Chair Car, with a capacity of 70 or so, during 1995 and instead provided a so called First Class bogie, with a seating capacity of 70 or so.

Thus an AC sitting bogie was replaced with a non-AC sitting bogie, with equal capacity. That First Class bogie which had only seating facility, was in no way comparable with the normal First Class facility, which had wider seats and with much lesser seats (28) and offering the passengers an option to sleep in the wide berths, warranting higher costing, in comparison with an AC Chair Car seat. Since the bogie had been categorised as First Class, probably meant for local travel not exceeding 1 hr., Indian Railways started charging higher fare, while providing an inferior service to the travelling public. The so called First Class bogie and the tariff might have been appropriate, for short distances, as in the case of suburban train service. Since the Railways did not respond to our complaint, we approached the National Commission, for deficient service rendered. Unfortunately, the National Commission took a narrow view that matters pertaining to tariff fixing was beyond the jurisdiction of the consumer court.

So, we approached the Supreme Court, for the first time in 1999. In spite of all the relevant arguments placed by me, the Supreme Court bench was not keen to take up the issue placed before them. As stated earlier, without due diligence we had never filed the cases in a hurry. I have always been keen to safeguard the reputation of the Council over the years, and was always for justice and fair play. Further, our resources were too limited to venture on any mindless adventure. Providing a service in a "deficient" manner, while collecting higher charges is fundamentally an unfair trade practice and needs to be hauled up. When the service provider (Indian Railways) provided convenience and comfort less than an AC Chair Car and charged at a higher rate, as though the passenger was being provided facilities similar to a First Class travel, it definitely amounted to an unfair trade practice, which could have been adjudicated under the Consumer Protection Act.

Why those in the judicial bodies, with a long exposure to law and justice, could not appreciate this fundamental interpretation of law is beyond my comprehension. So, thereafter, I wrote to the then Chief Justice of India, Dr. Justice A.S.Anand, about the injustice done to our appeal in the Supreme Court. To my pleasant surprise, after some time the AC Chair Car was restored in place of the so called First Class. So, *as an activist, one can hardly ever afford to close an issue without any conviction.*

Creating faith & confidence

The purpose, with which we had pursued Council activities, instilled confidence among Rourkela residents and gave them hope that if they ever faced injustice (either in terms of defective goods or deficient service) as a consumer, they could turn to our organisation for support.

This faith and confidence resulted in a lot of individual cases getting resolved in an amicable manner, by the concerned individuals themselves. Often, I used to hear from housewives and others that they had visited such and such shop. They had suspected foul play in pricing or other issues. At that point they had uttered the name of the Council and that they would approach us for the defective good or deficiency in service. Thereafter, the shopkeeper used to resolve the issue in an amicable manner. So, each and everyone had developed a confidence to tackle the problem faced by him/her, as a consumer. Being a smaller city also helped the cause.

The LPG under-weighing case

The overall general awareness on consumer rights and laws rose within the Steel Township due to Council's initiatives since 1985. It is because of this general awareness that we could create, one Sunday morning in 2000, one of the residents of the Steel Township met me when I was meeting the public in the Council's office. He informed me that the *'Indane'* LPG refill he received had only about 8 kg of LPG, as against the prescribed weight of 14.2 kg, but the dealer had not replaced the short-filled refill, in spite of complaining a couple of times and the other refill in use also could get exhausted and hence the urgency to get the replacement. He also informed that he had ascertained the shortfall through a German made spring balance available in his house. Since a complaint of this nature is serious, without just going by his written complaint, I arranged for a visit to his house to confirm the allegations made. (***First lesson for any activist or even a consumer. Never go by hearsay. See for yourself and confirm, so that your efforts are fruitful at the end.***) During my visit I found that whatever he alleged was indeed true. The refill cylinder did have the seal intact. Having confirmed the short-filling, I talked to the *'Indane'* dealer and asked him as to why he had not replaced the short-filled refill. As is the standard excuse, he blamed the complainant consumer of having misbehaved with him. Anyhow, he assured that he would replace the short-filled refill as desired by me. After about a week or so, the complainant consumer, Mr. Mohapatra visited our office to thank me for my intervention. However, the passing comment he made, while leaving our office simply baffled me. He informed that he had received two refill cylinders, of which one was short by 0.5 kg and the other by 1 kg. Since they were comparatively better than what had happened previously, he had accepted those cylinders. That sparked my thinking that something could be wrong with the weight of LPG refills being supplied to the consumers. To prove or disprove this theory, we decided to conduct a random survey in the Steel Township, and ascertain whether there was any abnormality in the weight of the LPG refills supplied, as an overwhelming majority of the residents depended on '*Indane*' gas. Our Joint Secretary during that time, Mr. B.Panda was entrusted with that survey.

Random sample survey

The survey covered randomly chosen 48 households of '*Indane*' consumers of the Steel Township, between 14th – 20th June 2000. On weighment of filled and sealed refills, it was found that the refills on an average contained only 12.74 kg (10.3% or 1.46 kg less), thereby inflicting a loss of Rs. 24/- per refill, while the refill was being sold at Rs. 253/-.

Indian Oil Corporation (IOC) as well as the ministry of Consumer Affairs, Government of India, including the Director (Legal Metrology) were informed and requested to act. On account of this, IOC offered to conduct a joint survey.

The Joint Survey with the participation of Mr. B.Panda, Jt. Secretary, of the Council, along with the Asst. Manager (LPG), IOC, Mr. B.Minz, was conducted, on 22nd July 2000. They weighed filled refills in 18 households. The weighed refills on an average contained only 12.59 kg (11.33% or 1.61 kg less). Since the outcome was worse than even our own independent findings, they excused themselves mid-way through the survey and did not even sign the papers.

Semi-automated Carousel Machine - the Culprit

IOC kept assuring that their LPG bottling plants were fine and wanted this author, who was then the Secretary of the Council, to visit their plant for a first-hand knowledge. The author being a qualified Industrial Engineer, habituated to routinely studying process/plant bottlenecks, on his visit in August 2000, in no time assessed that the bottling plant consisting of its semi-automated carousel machine was the root cause of the problem. The information was shared with the Plant Manager then and there. But he confidently said that all IOC's LPG bottling plants, numbering 120, had similar machinery. This fact further motivated me to take up the issue with all the more seriousness, as the entire country was being affected due to the casualness of the IOCL. What is all the more baffling is that IOCL being one of the Fortune 500 companies was recruiting their engineers from some of the best institutions of the country.

If something serious like a big lacunae in the LPG filling can be easily understood by a casual visitor like me within 30 mins, how were the best paid engineers and technologists who handled such plants each day were not able to figure out even after continuous exposure? The answer, I believe, is probably the IOCL engineers or the management was not keen to set right the systemic deficiencies or upgrade, as it would be cost intensive and require their initiative. Further, the affected housewives were in no position to even know that they were being supplied less, as weighing such a heavy item was not that easy and the company that supplied them the refill was a government owned public sector undertaking, which they trusted.

The Company was not willing to accept the fault nor was willing to discuss about a solution. After giving sufficient time and even highlighting this problem in the Central Consumer Protection Council, a case was filed in July 2001, before the National Consumer Disputes Redressal Commission (NCDRC), as the loss inflicted on the consumers by IOC was estimated to be Rs. 750 crores per year.

Though, the National Commission in principle agreed to consider our Original Petition (No. 224 of 2001), things were actually not moving forward for about an year (remember, that under the Consumer Protection Act, disputes are supposed to be resolved within 180 days max., when requiring detailed examination). Then, in August 2002, to nudge the Commission into action, I filed a "Declaration" sworn by an experienced electronic engineer, familiar with online weighing systems, Mr. Umakanta Mishra, one of my esteemed colleague and friend of the Steel Plant, that it is possible to automate the carousel machine so as to eliminate the manually cumbersome tare neutralisation process, within a reasonable cost of Rs. 15 lakhs per machine. As expected, that initiative worked and thereafter in December 2002, the Commission appointed the Professors of IIT, Kharagpur to study the Balasore LPG Bottling Plant, in Orissa, supplying the LPG refills to Rourkela, and confirm whether it is capable of delivering the LPG refills within the prescribed norms of 14.2 kg ± 150 gm. So, sometimes, on technical issues as a complainant/appellant, one may have to even nudge the bench towards appropriate direction. But, even such nudging sometimes does not succeed as I experienced in the Supreme Court. More about that in the next chapter "***LPG under-weighment case exposes the fallibility of the Supreme Court***".

Amendments to the Consumer Protection Act introduced

While the case was being heard by the NCDRC, the Consumer Protection Act was amended, effective from 15th March 2003. Several important provisions which were relevant to this case, especially for awarding punitive damages, payment of penalty when the defective good or deficient service affects large number of consumers, providing adequate cost to the litigant, etc. were introduced and the Council in January 2004 itself, sought the invocation of those provisions in this case.

The consumers who approached the consumer courts, after lot of delays and expenses found that they were finally getting a pittance after all the efforts. Hence, the Consumer Protection Act, under sec. 14(1)(d) provided power to the District Forum to grant punitive damages. Section 14(1)(hb) empowers the Consumer Court to direct the Opposite Party to pay a minimum of 5% of the value of defective goods sold or deficient services provided (please note that it is not the actual loss or shortfall, but the cost of the goods itself, which need to be considered), if the goods or services had affected large number of consumers not identifiable conveniently. Similarly, another newly introduced provision (14(1)(r)) provided for awarding adequate costs to parties.

These progressive consumer friendly provisions have the potential to totally eliminate the Unfair Trade Practices. Unfortunately, till date, these progressive provisions have remained only on paper. At least, I am not aware of any case wherein these provisions were invoked by the consumer courts. It is an irony that in the proposed CP Act amendment bill of 2012, which is now placed before the Parliament Select Committee, the minimum penalty has been enhanced from 5% to 25%. Indian political hypocrisy at its best.

Professors of IIT, Kharagpur concur with the Council

After studying the system, observing the filling process and collecting adequate data, as per statistical requirements, Professors of IIT found that the LPG Bottling Plant was incapable of filling and delivering the right quantity of LPG to the consumers.

After they reported in July 2003, Government of India, not to be left behind, constituted a Committee, under Additional Secretary, Consumer Affairs, on 11th September 2003, to identify problems relating to short filling of LPG in domestic cylinders and to suggest suitable remedial measures. I was also nominated to that Committee, in addition to representatives of all the three Oil Marketing Companies. Director, Legal Metrology, was its Member Secretary.

The Committee constituted by the Department of Consumer Affairs, Government of India in their Report, in March 2005, concluded the immediate need for modernisation of the bottling plants.

National Commission (NCDRC) directs pre-delivery weighing in consumer's presence

The NCDRC, based on the findings of the Professors of IIT, Kharagpur, and the Committee set up by the Ministry of Consumer Affairs, Government of India, concluded in October 2005 that in the prevailing LPG bottling system, consumers could get less than the stipulated weight of 14.2 kg and hence as an interim measure *directed IOC to adopt pre-delivery weight checking of the LPG refill at the consumer's premises and also to publicise that initiative through advertisements in the media, in a prominent manner,* as was done by Hindustan Petroleum Corporation.

IOC did not comply with the 2005 directives and NCDRC took on record such behaviour, in 2006 as well as in 2007, at the instance of the Complainant Council. But the final order of the NCDRC passed in July 2007 glossed over IOC's remiss behaviour and Council's prayers for awards for damages as per the amended Act. It did not even discuss about that in the final order. The Council promptly appealed for a Review of the Order of the NCDRC, as it had not addressed its prayers for compensation.

After 10 years, National Commission concedes that it could not examine the case

The Council's review before the NCDRC evoked the following admissions by the NCDRC in 2010: "*Applying this ratio to the facts of present case, we are of the view that the review application for consideration/ grant of said prayer (d), which will be deemed to have been declined, is not maintainable under Section 22(2) of the Act. Otherwise also this would require detailed examination of the case which is impermissible under Section 22(2) of the Act. Application is dismissed as such. It will be open to the complainant to have redressal of its grievance as may be permissible under the law.*" Who *prevented the Commission from examining the case, after having dealt it for 10 years? - is a pertinent question which could arise in anyone's mind.*

A delay of 1,071 days condoned by the Supreme Court

Since the NCDRC's response was not found justified, the Council appealed to the Supreme Court in 2010 against the final order of the NCDRC made in July 2007, after a delay of 1,071 days. The case was heard by Justice G.S.Singhvi and Justice S.J.Mukhopadhaya. While the Supreme Court condoned the delay of 1,071 days, obviously because of the review proceedings in the NCDRC contributing to the delay, it failed to address the issues raised in the appeal, which were until now not addressed by the NCDRC. The judgment of the Supreme Court said that the appeal was 'infructuous' as both the government and IOC had complied with the order of the NCDRC. *How the Judges came to this grossly wrong conclusion about the subject of the appeal is indeed appalling, as even an unqualified lawyer would not had difficulty in understanding the grounds of appeal.*

The basic question as to why a delay of 1071 days was condoned will obviously demonstrate the glaring error in the judgment. The huge delay was condoned because the Council had sought a legal review of the order of the National Commission for the apparent errors, including but not limited to non-invoking the provision of Sec. 14(1)(hb), etc. of the Consumer Protection Act after having concluded that a large number of consumers were affected by the under-weighed refills delivered by IOC. But the judgment, after having observed that the appeal was against the order of the National Commission, failed to discuss the order in any manner. Instead, the impugned judgment discussed the compliance part of the government and the oil marketing companies, which was not the reason for which the appeal had been filed.

Incidentally, on 16.10.2012, when the instant appeal was being heard, finding that the bench was missing the real issues and was concentrating elsewhere relating to pre-delivery checking, filling of equal weighted refill cylinders, methodology to know the content of the cylinder by pressure gauge, printing of right type of Receipts by the dealers and so on, I had intervened to say that the appeal was mainly relating to non-invoking of certain important provisions of the Consumer Protection Act, namely, Sec. 14(1)(d), 14(1)(hb) and 14(1)(i) and that the National Commission had already taken care of the under-weighing problem by ordering for automation of the LPG bottling plants. *Hon'ble Justice G.S.Singhvi specifically assured that all these would be discussed in the final order.*

Further, I had also referred to a recent judgment of the Supreme Court, *M/s Nagpur Golden Transport Company (Regd.) Versus M/s Nath Traders & Ors., Civil Appeal No. 3546 of 2006, involving the scrap value of motors worth Rs. 3 lakhs, amounting to less than Rs. 1 lakh.* Even for such a nominal value of the goods involved, the Supreme Court termed it as "undue enrichment" and ordered that value should be compensated. Whereas in the instant case, more than Rs. 65,000 crores worth of under-weighed LPG refills were involved, till 2005, I argued. *At this Hon'ble Justice G.S.Singhvi had even remarked (in the open Court) that the undersigned should become a lawyer.* (*But somehow, based on the news item of PTI the next day, all the newspapers across the country published an article that the Supreme Court had issued directives to advertise so that consumers may insist on pre-delivery weighing of the LPG refills.* **What a pity, that the Supreme Court should take credit for something which the NCDRC had directed more than 7 years before. Interestingly, this well publicised directive of the Supreme Court did not find a mention in the final judgment.** One can well conclude that making observations as per convenience has become the order of the day. MAY GOD SAVE THIS COUNTRY!

This, in addition to the Statement of the Case, Rejoinder and Supplementary Rejoinder to the Counter Affidavits were filed by the Appellant Council, during the course of the hearing and the last one (Additional Supplementary Rejoinder) was not taken on record in spite of the undersigned pleading for allowing him to submit the same on 5th Dec. 2012. In all these documents the Appellant repeatedly prayed for considering the original prayers which were omitted by the National Commission without even a discussion.

How can an Appeal filed under sec. 23, become infructuous?

When an individual is dissatisfied with the order of the National Commission, he appeals to the Supreme Court, under Section 23 of the Consumer Protection Act. The Supreme Court has to conclude only whether the NCDRC order is maintainable or not, based on the facts placed before it. No appeal can become 'infructuous' unless it is filed under Section 27A, where the implementation part is involved.

The Supreme Court also dismissed the review sought by the Council. If the judiciary fails the consumers, where will they go? *The apex court was probably finding the issues raised were too big and the issues relating to "punitive* damages" had to be addressed for the first time, under the Consumer Protection Act and that too against a state undertaking. A cumulative value of Rs 65,000 crore of short-weighed cooking gas refills had been sold by IOC until 2005, the time when an interim order was passed, warranting IOC to pay at least Rs 3,250 crore to the Consumer Welfare Fund, as per the existing Consumer Protection Rules, which itself is questionable.

All 184 LPG Bottling Plants Modernised

Seldom a voluntary consumer organisation could take up such a major issue, prove it technically correct and provide tangible relief to crores of unsuspecting housewives across the country. Today, all the 184 bottling plants, of the three oil marketing companies (IOC, BPCL and HPCL) have been automated. The government (Petroleum & Natural Gas ministry) is supposed to have spent around Rs 300 crores for this modernisation. Unfortunately, the apex court of the country has not provided relief as mandated by the law, to the consumer organisation and the consumers, who relentlessly pursued the matter for over 14 years.

So, a Fortune 500 Company after deceiving the consumers for several decades and having successfully adopted an Unfair Trade Practice, supplying Rs 65,000 crore worth of short-weighed cooking gas refills to the unsuspecting housewives, has walked scot-free. Thanks to the ineffective apex court, the consumers and the consumer organisation, which took up the issue, have been left high and dry.

A sad truth that emerges is that even the highest Court of the country does not deliver justice, laws do not serve the purpose for which they are made, whimsical decisions of the judiciary remain unquestioned and the people of this great nation will stand to suffer for more time to come. This depressing conclusion is derived as even the preceding Chief Justice of India (CJI) was informed about this gross injustice done to the consumer movement in Feb. 2013 itself, after the Appeal for Review was also turned down. This author is yet to receive even an acknowledgment, leave alone any action. Not to leave any stone unturned, we filed a Curative Petition, a rare one for a voluntary organisation. After its dismissal in a routine manner, I once again wrote to the then CJI, in July 2014 (please refer Annexure-B), with zero result.

Chapter – IV

LPG Under-Weighment Case Exposes the Fallibility of the Supreme Court

Supreme Court is the last resort for those who seek justice in all matters concerning their life and property. Over 125 crore Indians look up to this body as an embodiment of legal knowledge, wisdom and power, to safeguard their interests and the society and act without fear or favour in the job entrusted to them. If the Supreme Court fails to be professional and gives an impression that it is whimsical and lacks diligence in the dispensation of justice, it can cause immense damage to the Indian democracy.

Legal luminaries say that to err is human. However, when a matter is decided by the Supreme Court, there is no further appeal against its judgment. The principle of finality of a judgment is an important element in the administration of justice. The principle of finality is insisted upon, not because the judgment of the apex court is infallible but because, a final decision on merits in a litigation between the parties is supposed to sub serve the maxim-*interest reipublicae ut sit finis litium*, which in simple language means that it is in the interest of the State that there should be an end to litigation. Having said that will it not be cruel to allow the totally irrelevant and whimsical judgements to go unquestioned?

In order to remedy miscarriage of justice, the review is provided, say the enlightened advocates of the bar. Further it is said that the power of review is exercised when there is an error apparent on the face of the record. They also agree that a court can generally not be easily persuaded to believe that its view was erroneous and so in a vast majority of cases review petitions are dismissed. For the review petitions that are accepted and where the judicial conscience of the Bench which pronounced the judgment under review is pricked, the court does not stand on its ego but acknowledges its error and gives the requisite relief, they add with pride. But this window of opportunity appears to arise in rarest of rare cases and that too when constitutional bodies or government prefer such Reviews or Curative Petitions.

Let us now consider how the humungous efforts of Consumer Protection Council, Rourkela, to bring to book one of the mega scandals of independent India went uncompensated, against the provisions of the Consumer Protection Act, with the Supreme Court being a significant contributor. When such things happen, one wonders whether it will be appropriate to term it as a human error or a blunder of huge proportions.

The Council filed the Original Petition against M/s IOCL for supplying under-weighed LPG refills to the consumers across the country, in the National Consumer Disputes Redressal Commission, New Delhi, in 2001 (O.P. No. 224 of 2001). After a thorough investigation and certification by the Professors of IIT, Kharagpur and the Department of Consumer Affairs, Government of India, the National Commission, concurring with the findings of the Council, directed the upgradation of all the 184 LPG bottling plants, in which tare neutralisation of the refills were being manually done. The National Commission though ordered relief to the consumers at large, without any elaboration failed to consider or record its order on Prayer (d) of the Council, which was for award of 1% of the estimated loss of Rs. 750 crores suffered by the consumers in a year, in the Original Petition filed in 2001. After the amendments incorporated in the Consumer Protection Act, in 2003, in line with the provisions of the Act, the prayer (d) was enhanced to 5%.

Since the National Commission had overlooked one of the important prayers submitted before it though the Act specifically provided for it, the Council filed for a Review before the National Commission. Though the matter could have been decided by circulation, the Review Petition was heard over 10 sittings and lingered on for nearly 3 years. Finally, the National Commission, in August 2010, indirectly agreed to the shortcoming in its Order and observed as under:

"...we are of the view that review application for consideration/grant of said prayer (d) which will be deemed to have been declined, is not maintainable under

Section 22(2) of the Act. Otherwise also this would require detailed examination of the case which is impermissible under Section 22(2) of the Act. Application is dismissed as such. It will be open to the complainant to have redressal of its grievance as may be permissible under the law."

Since the value of the defective goods (under-weighed LPG refills) involved is about Rs. 65,000 crores and the specified penalty as per the Act is a minimum of Rs. 3,250 crores, it was thought that the National Commission was probably not keen to address such a massive issue, and subsequently an appeal was filed before the Supreme Court (Civil Appeal No. 10126 of 2010).

We in the Council quite conscious that we have to place the exact facts before the apex court to avoid wastage of time of the presiding officers (judges), have been harping on the issues we sought the adjudication, right from the 'Listing Performa', as under:

"15. Point of law and question of law raised in the case:

- *Whether the Amended provisions of the Consumer Protection Act, which became effective from 15.03.2003, are applicable to the present case, though filed in 2001, as the cause of action continued to exist even till 2007.*

- *Once the Forum (National Commission) concludes that a large number of consumers suffered loss, across the country, is it not mandatory on its part to invoke Sec. 14(1)(hb)?*

- *When should the Commission below invoke the provisions of Sec. 14(1) (d), and award punitive damages?*

- *What is the reasonable cost envisaged under Sec. 14(1)(i)"*

Though the Civil Appeal was accepted for detailed examination, without any hesitation, in the first hearing itself, in 2010, by the bench comprising of Justice B.Sudershan Reddy and Justice S.S.Nijjar, all the problems started after the matter came up for hearing in 2012 before the bench comprising of Justice G.S.Singhvi and Justice S.J.Mukhopadhaya.

The time of the Supreme Court is precious and one would have expected the bench to come prepared with the issues raised before it for adjudication. Unfortunately, that was not to be. Even after 4-5 sittings there was no change in the *status quo*.

On 16th Oct. 2012, when this author, appearing for the Appellant Council found that the bench was continuing to discuss about various aspects not relating to the issues for which the Appeal had been filed, intervened to guide them that the Appeal had been necessitated for determining the award of compensation under Section 14(1)(hb) of the Consumer Protection Act, as the National Commission had failed to adjudicate on this issue. In that connection this author also quoted the judgement of the Supreme Court, in M/s Nagpur Golden Transport Company (Regd.) Vs M/s Nath Traders & Ors., Civil Appeal No. 3546 of 2006, in which for a nominal sum of Rs. 1 lakh or so, value of damaged mono-block pumps, the case traversed from District Forum to Supreme Court and it held that it was a case of undue enrichment and the respondent was directed to pay the amount to the appellant. Whereas the instant case involved Rs. 65,000 crores worth of goods. To this, Justice Singhvi immediately remarked that this author should become a lawyer. In another instance he also remarked that environmental degradation is a much serious issue and in Punjab water levels had gone very low, say, below 250 feet and the author should take up environmental issues. Those were probably the ominous indicators that the bench was not going to adjudicate upon the issues for which the Appeal was filed. Since I fully trusted the apex court, I failed to read between the lines.

Though all these discussions were held on 16th Oct., the "Record of Proceedings" of the Court recorded as below:

"We have heard Shri B. Vaidyanathan, the appellant appearing in person, Shri P.P.Malhotra, learned Additional Solicitor General and Shri Parag P. Tripathi, learned senior counsel appearing on behalf of the Indian Oil Corporation Limited and perused the record.

Shri Malhotra and Shri Tripathi say that they will hold consultation with the concerned functionaries of the government and Oil Companies and come out with concrete suggestions on the issues of checking weight of cylinders and the gas and giving wide publicity in print and electronic media about the rights of the consumers to be supplied LPG gas of particular weight.

Shri Malhotra and Shri Tripathi further say that they would also hold consultation on the issue of obtaining cylinders by the Oil Companies of the standard specification so that the consumers may not be misled about the weight of the empty cylinders and the quantity of gas."

Recording of the proceedings verbatim is not expected. But an honest reproduction of all that happened is what one expects from such a premier body, which survives on the hard earned tax payers' money. Unfortunately honesty is in premium in a country, which dreams of ruling the 21st century.

But on 5th Dec. 2012, the next date of hearing in the impugned case, the hearing started with dictation of the order, without discussing whatever was already ordered, which startlingly concluded that the matter brought by the Council was infructuous.

Infructuous means unfruitful or unprofitable. How a case filed for adjudication of an issue of law, without even being discussed upon can become unfruitful, unless the bench entrusted with the job of adjudicating prefers to record as per its whims and conclude contrary to the facts placed on record and discussed in the court. Very sad and pathetic state of affairs indeed. While the bench would have been fully justified to negate the prayers of the Appellant Council, on valid grounds, it is travesty of justice to pass and penalise a voluntary organisation surviving on meagre resources, for having come to it, just because it did not want to adjudicate on an issue of law about which either it did not have sufficient knowledge or the issue being too big to be of comfort to it.

When an individual is dissatisfied with the order of the National Commission, he appeals to the Supreme Court, under Section 23 of the Consumer Protection Act. The Supreme Court has to conclude only whether the NCDRC order is maintainable or not, based on the facts placed before it. No appeal can become 'infructuous' unless it is filed under Section 27A, where the implementation part is involved.

Since we in the Council still believed that some mishap had happened due to oversight or whatever, exhausted our option for seeking a Review, which was promptly dismissed. Still not convinced, the Council moved the Curative Petition in 2013 and the same got formally dismissed in July 2014, without a discussion. Readers need to know that to file the Curative Petition, it needs to be certified by a designated Senior Advocate of the Supreme Court, that in the interest of justice the case needs to be reconsidered for reasons which are to be recorded.

After all this, if still gaping holes exist in the dispensation of justice, the higher judiciary needs to do some soul searching. Since every concerned party, whether it be the media or the executive have their own axe to grind and are hardly in a position to discuss such aberrations in an objective manner, people of this great nation are being left to the mercy of these demi gods of justice in the supreme judiciary.

The reader could be interested to know whether the modernisation of the LPG Bottling Plants made any difference to the paying public. I was also eager to know this. Accordingly, I had arranged for conducting random sample surveys both at Chennai and Rourkela, during the 3rd and 4th quarters of 2012. The entire effort was in a way to inform the not so enthusiastic Supreme Court bench that our initiatives had indeed turned around the under-weighing issue.

While at Chennai, out of the 53 households utilising *Indane* surveyed, a healthy 66% (35 nos.) were in possession of refills, which were having LPG within the norms (14.2 ± 0.15 kg) and the overall average deviation of the 53 refills studied was 50 gms (ie., the consumers received 50 gms above the norms).

Whereas, the survey at Rourkela was not that flattering. Though the survey revealed an increase in the number of refills which had LPG within the norms, from 12.5% (survey done in 2000) to 40.7%, it was much less in comparison to our finding at Chennai. Similarly, the overall average weight was short by 0.6 kg, though could be better compared to our study finding of 1.46 kg less, in 2000, indicating that there is still a vast scope for improvement, even in comparison with Chennai finding. As a matter of fact, while the Chennai households showed a reasonable random variations on either side of the stipulated weight of 14.2 kg, the Rourkela finding pointed towards a one sided deviation, with hardly any positive deviations. This might be something to do with the Plant settings, catering to smaller cities and towns, in comparison to those Plants, catering to metros like Chennai, which are politically more important.

Unfortunately, with the indifference of the apex court being so evident to even address the basic issues for which we approached it, consumer organisations like ours, will hardly be motivated to repeatedly approach it for further redressals.

Chapter – V

Funding – a Perennial Problem

Voluntary movements, in general, in our country, especially the consumer movement and the voluntary consumer organisations have all along been suffering for want of resources. Except a handful who have the ability and the knack to tap international funding agencies, smaller organisations like ours have always sustained with enormous amount of balancing and tight rope walking, in respect of financial resources. Rather, a prime mover like me, as in the case of the Consumer Protection Council, Rourkela, had the onerous responsibility of somehow managing the show, by not only offering many types of services free of cost to the Council and consumers but also by chipping in with sizeable financial contribution(s), year after year.

As a matter of fact, between 1994-95 and 2007-08, my personal financial contribution was about Rs. 3 lakhs, working out on an average to Rs. 25,000/- per year, for which I claimed income tax rebate as well. Similarly, even after leaving Rourkela, as Chief Mentor of the Council, I had to incur all the expenses related to National Commission and Supreme Court cases and other activities performed by me, commencing from April 2008 to date, amounting to over Rs. 4.3 lakhs. We in the Council recently received a grant of Rs. 4.73 lakhs (the amount we sought), as reimbursement for the expenses incurred in the LPG under-weighing case, over a period of 15 years, from the CWF (Consumer Welfare Fund), administered by the Department of Consumer Affairs, Government of India, and I will get my dues. But, investing so much without interest, for so many years, could be a challenge for many. I have stated this fact not to boast of the donations nor the interest free loan that I have offered to a cause and an organisation, which I enjoyed working for, but to highlight the plight of these organisations in making both ends meet. Unfortunately, while grants are sanctioned for the establishment of a facility, the Government of India is yet to feel the need to support such ventures on a long term for achieving the objectives. For example, the Ministry of Consumer Affairs, Government of India, sanctioned us a project for establishing a Consumer Information Centre (CIC), at Rourkela, with an outlay of Rs. 3 lakhs or so in the year 1999-2000. The Centre was established with a rented accommodation, comprising of a library, with a decent collection of consumer related books and journals like CPJ (Consumer Protection Judgments), CPR (Consumer Protection Reporter), and SCALE (Scale), a facility for counselling consumers and a computer system. Though SAIL (Steel Authority of India Ltd.), Rourkela Steel Plant, was kind enough to oblige us by providing a slightly damaged quarter on a nominal rent, with electricity and water charges on par with the market rate, even that expenditure along with maintenance and caretaker salary works out to Rs. 30,000 to Rs. 35,000 per year. This is very nominal when compared with bigger cities, but there is no provision or support to incur even this expenditure from the government, the sponsor of the Centre. Consequently, as of date, the Council owes about Rs. 58,000/- (as on Feb. '17) to the Steel Plant, towards rent, electricity and water charges, for the CIC premises. Our Information Centre is still alive and those who followed me as Secretary have all been trying their best to keep it going. The only telephone that was there has been surrendered to cut cost, within a couple of years of my leaving Rourkela. *No one should be surprised, if the organisers are forced to shut down the shop (Council), for want of resources.*

When a voluntary organisation charges even a nominal fee for the services they render, quite often than not, it gives rise to criticisms from several quarters that the organisation is doing a business and some even allege that the office-bearers are minting money for their own welfare. Here, I wish to quote an incident which appeared in the press about a leading consumer organisation of Chennai in the 90s that it was collecting money for appearing in the courts and a consumer forum had even questioned that. We are a nation of poor, habituated to subsidies and it will be appropriate if the voluntary organisations extend their services free of cost, but how will they sustain after doing everything free is something for which I have not been able to find a convincing answer.

But for the LML and APSL cases, which we fought in the National Commission on behalf of nearly 1800 complainants, we have not even appealed individually for financial support (donation) for sustaining their cases. In those two cases, I did make a personal appeal to the complainants to contribute at least Rs. 50/- so as to cover our expenses of going to Delhi and fighting the case. Though, good majority of the complainants donated Rs. 50/- or more as solicited, there were individuals who did not contribute also. Keeping these issues in mind and to safeguard our image, we never demanded donations, unless it was made voluntarily, for lodging complaints or for pursuing their cases in the court. Unless this funding issue which threatens the healthy survival of the voluntary consumer organisations can be addressed effectively, even genuine organisations' existence and their ability to perform will be under constant threat.

To bridge this gap, the government with its vast machinery needs to frame policies that are realistic and sustainable.

At this juncture, I am sure, the readers would have concluded that working for a cause is indeed challenging and requires loads of commitment, tenacity and skill sets essential for initiating and obtaining grants from government and its agencies. This is more so for those who do not want to compromise on their integrity. With the recent changes in funding NGOs, being regulated by enforcing registration in the *Niti Ayog's* website "*Darpan*" and making payment only through PFMS (Public Financial Management System), manipulative sanctions and payments have all been made all the more difficult. Transparent systems could pose some problem initially for the law abiding citizens, but it is after all the best way to plug leakage of public funds. So, have the zeal, commitment, and the skills, your NGO can still survive.

Chapter – VI

Way Forward

As an organisation to promote consumer awareness, I believed that instead of giving sermons, we need to take up individual complaints and solve them to instil confidence in the people that systems do exist and if we can take up our issues in an appropriate manner, it can be resolved. It is in this direction that we encouraged individuals to file their complaints with our Council so that the disputes are resolved, grievances are redressed, pertaining to defective goods or deficient services.

During my journey of over 22 years, ever since we started our Council, on 8th September 1985, till I left Rourkela in April 2008, I as the Secretary of the Council and as the principal volunteer, had dealt with over 5000 individual complaints and consumer court as well as a few Supreme Court cases, overwhelming majority of which were resolved. That experience had exposed me to both positive and not so positive and wrong approach of the individuals. While on the positive side, I did come across individuals, though lesser in number, who were voluntarily willing to share the benefits of the Council's initiative; more numbers at least acknowledged the Council's role in a positive manner, may be by joining our organisation as a Life Member or by making a nominal donation. There were also instances when some consumers without even understanding the voluntary nature of the services that were extended, totally on honorary basis, had unrealistic expectations and non-cooperative mind-set. But on the whole, the fulfilling experience of having been able to be of help to the people at large, overwhelming majority of whom were gullible and ignorant, and being an instrument in resolving major issues of relevance in day-to-day life, gave me the satisfaction and kept me going. In those individual cases which we could resolve, some experiences stand out and I am able to recollect some of them. These examples which are narrated here should be able to educate the consumers as to how they should not behave if they are indeed eager to assert their respect and sovereignty.

We had filed a case, one of the first cases, against a drycleaner, who was supposed to have damaged a saree. The case was fought in the District Forum, at Sundergarh (100 km from Rourkela) and we won. The Forum directed the drycleaner to pay some compensation. The aggrieved individual who hardly knew anything about the consumer court, nor in a position to get anything from the drycleaner, directly approached the Forum without even consulting us, after we won the case for him, as there was some delay in the execution of the order (Firing from someone else's shoulder!). By doing so, he had done no credit to himself or the organisation which had taken up his case *'free of cost'*.

Sometimes the greed of the consumer puts him in all difficulties. An employee of SAIL, Rourkela Steel Plant, who is not educated, wanted some cash for his household expenses. He was probably misguided by some unscrupulous elements that the banks extend consumer durable loans and he can easily get that, provided, he is able to produce the bills/invoice from a shopkeeper, who is willing to sell the good to him. The poor fellow went to an unethical trader, with the understanding that he would give a cheque for Rs. 25,000/- and that the trader should give him the cash, after taking his commission. The bank issued a cheque in the name of the trader and the trader neither gave him the cash nor the articles. Considering the educational background and the financial condition of the concerned individual, we took up his case. The District Forum promptly awarded him due compensation and cost. Since there was problem in executing the order of the Forum, keeping our reputation in mind, in a rare gesture, the President of the District Forum himself, personally approached the shopkeeper, with the Police in tow and arranged for the dues, as per his order. So, be ethical in your dealings and do not fall prey to temptations of easy money or wealth (oft repeated wisdom!!).

In Orissa, Ration Shops were being managed by private individuals and hence many of those shops were either totally shut for most of the time or open partially in a day. This is in contrast to the ration shops in Tamilnadu, which are managed by cooperative societies and are kept open on a regular basis every day, with fixed working hours. A complaint was received from a well-educated individual that the ration shop had not issued him sugar during a particular month. As per our standard practice, I wrote a complaint to the Assistant Civil

Supplies Officer (ACSO), informing about that ration shop. After about a week or so, I had some work and had to visit the office of the Additional District Magistrate (ADM), Rourkela. I met the ADM in person and in the course of the meeting, he started charging me that he is informed that we were making fake complaints. I was shocked when he said like that and enquired as to what was the matter. Then he smiled, being seasoned, and told me that I had complained about non-issue of sugar by a ration shop, whereas he was having documents to show that sugar was actually issued to the particular complainant. May be, he had understood the game. I informed him that only based on a written complaint, I had sent the letter to the ACSO. Later, when I enquired from the complainant, he coolly said that after he lodged his complaint with the Council, the ration shop owner visited his house and pleaded with him to accept the sugar and told him whether he wanted him to lose his dealership because of him. So, he had to accept the sugar without even bothering to inform me. He felt sorry for whatever happened. The fundamental lesson is if individuals are keen to complain, they should be ready to go through the process. Then only systems would improve. If one is not sure of defending his own complaint, made on solid grounds, it would be better to leave everything to fate and suffer silently. Rather, it would be appropriate to consider that one among them is taking the lead and is willing to execute the onerous task on their behalf, *'free of cost'*.

In the last 3 decades, ever since consumer protection came to get the recognition that was due from the Government of India and its enactment of the all-important Consumer Protection Act, the market scenario has undergone very positive changes. Thanks to the liberalisation of the economy, competition in the market place, proliferation of the internet and communication technology, things have become much better for an average consumer. Add to this the introduction of the regulatory mechanism in Insurance, Electricity, Communication and the rapid digitisation of financial transactions, consumers are getting better protected. Competition in the market place is the best friend of the common man. Because of this competition, consumers have a choice in almost everything they buy, whether it be white goods such as the refrigerator, TV, motorcycle or even FMCG (Fast Moving Consumer Goods) items such as toothpaste, shampoo or the toiletries. The competition has also resulted in withholding of the price line or even reduction in tariff, as is experienced in communication and electronics.

Because of the digitisation of the economy and proliferation of internet and mushrooming online shopping portals, shopping experience has undergone a qualitative change and the life has definitely eased. With leaders like *Amazon* entering the fray, consumers are now really having a "wow" experience, but the shoppers ought to exercise due diligence before making a purchase. It is better to be conservative in this regard rather than being compulsive and adventurous.

For those who lack experience, it will be better to consult those who already have the shopping experience, to know the pros and cons of utilising a particular shopping portal. One best way to assess a shopping portal is to search on 'Google' or such other search engines like 'Bing'. Invariably one will get lot of relevant information about the advantages and shortcomings of shopping on a portal and a feel of what other shoppers have to say about their experiences. This is true for even physical shops. One should have the habit of going through all the Terms and Conditions, as well as specifications of the product before making an online purchase. This practice will come in handy when you don't have the salesman or the shopkeeper around to answer your queries. Further, a wrong product will naturally be a wastage of time and money. One big advantage of prominent shopping portals is that there is ample feedback from the customers who had purchased the product, as to how beneficial that product is, its advantages and if it failed, and in which respect. I have always utilised such valuable feedback, while making my choice and invariably, such choices did work out fine.

One relevant point to note is that some of the feedbacks may relate to certain features about which we may not be concerned and it would be prudent to consider the overall assessment that you can derive from such feedbacks. This is more so because when we have sizeable number of (feedback) responses, everyone may not uniformly say that the product is excellent and some may talk about lesser important (comparatively) packaging was good and delivered within 24 hrs, rather than about the quality of the product. For example, when you want to purchase organic food items, some could feel that it is costly but quality is good. If you consider quality is of prime importance, though with a marginally higher cost, depending on the consumption pattern, one could even overlook the cost aspect. Similarly, for example, when you want a hacksaw for cutting wood and tree branch, in your household, what is important is its ability to cut wood, the grip, life and cost. If someone has informed that he tried to cut steel sheet and it did not work, it is naturally irrelevant to our need and hence need not be considered.

But, while purchasing clothing, one has to exercise utmost caution, as sizes and fitting vary from brand to brand. In a way, it would be better to go for known brands, about which we are familiar with. Still, there are many, especially the ladies, who feel that readymade clothing should be purchased only after physically wearing them, and getting them altered, especially the length of the pants, at the seller's premises itself. Returns policy is another important aspect, which one has to consider while making online purchases. Paying options are more or less standardised; i.e., cards, net banking or cash on delivery are available with almost all the portals. With the multiple verification processes in place (PIN number through mobile, email) and additional usage of security code while transacting in the payment gateway, have all made the internet shopping all the more safe and reliable. At the end of the successful transaction, it will be worth to note down or capture the web page with the transaction ID, so that in case of any need, the same can be referred. Caution is the watchword in Internet transactions, though instantaneous confirmation through SMS on mobile and email messages is the order of the day.

It is found that many gifting portals disappoint. Since these portals are having tie-up with local shops, ultimately, the quality of the product (cake, bouquets, etc.) and the delivery timing could sometimes go horribly wrong. At least make sure that the person to whom you have sent the gift, did receive the item and on time.

On the legal front, one important amendment to the Consumer Protection Act is in the pipeline. This amendment, which is being talked about for the last couple of years will come handy for those who procure goods from far off places. Right now, a consumer can file a case only in the District Forum or State Commission, in whose jurisdiction, the Opposite Party resides or carries on his business or has a branch office doing the same or similar business or where the cause of action arose. Thus, someone in Chennai, say, procures an item from Delhi, presently, as per the Act, if there is any dispute, he has to approach the District Forum, at Delhi, which is quite cumbersome and costly. Whereas the proposed amendment will enable the consumer to file his complaint at a District Forum, which is close to his residence or his place of work, though he might have purchased an item from a party whose establishment might be located far off from his residence. With the online shopping gaining momentum, with the proposed amendment in place, the consumer will stand better protected. The amendment is naturally expected to ensure better behaviour and concern to the paying public, by the sellers.

Last but not the least, knowing the weakness of the consumers for discounts, rebates and freebies, many online fly by night operators offer unbelievable deals. No one can protect you if you willingly fall for such cheap gimmicks. Be conservative; be informed; make a choice and deal with a reliable portal/site. Your interests will be fully protected.

Ominous portents: As someone who had been associated with the consumer movement, right from the days of enactment of the versatile Consumer Protection Act, I do feel that things have drifted badly, after the initial zeal and initiatives from the government. While the drift could be palpable right after the first decade of the Consumer Protection Act, it went unacceptably bad since 2006, when the Consumer Protection Rules were amended to castrate the Central Consumer Protection Council, the participative consultative body. Similarly, to eliminate the impact of section 14(1)(hb) of the Act (introduced in 2003), the Rules were enabled in 2004, to divert the entire benefits accruing from the invocation of sec. 14(1)(hb) to the Consumer Welfare Fund, so that no organisation or individual would take up seriously any rampant unfair trade practice affecting large groups of individuals.

Government's hands are full, due to inherent political lacunae, ineffective and genetically deformed administration, subjective and inefficient judiciary, ever growing population and unfulfilled needs, inequalities, historical caste curse, ever growing demands against inelastic resources, unfriendly neighbours, and many more. In such a scenario, those issues which are capable of making maximum noise and are considered to rupture even the existence of the government, are being given the importance, by the underequipped, fire-fighting mode administration. Consumer Protection being an welfare issue which does not attract international attention, may be as in the case of environment protection, or the local political attention as in the case of river water sharing or job reservation, there is hardly any interest from their end to promote Consumer Protection. Add to this the insignificant leadership of the consumer movement, whose sole objective appears to be conducting seminars and conferences to the tune of the sponsors, rather than addressing the grassroots issues to strengthen the consumer movement. As a matter of fact, when the Supreme Court dismissed the '*Indane*' under-weighment case, without even broaching the issues for which the Appeal was made by the Council, I personally appealed to the Consumer Coordination Council, a national level coalition of consumer organisations, in person, during their Annual General Meeting, in 2013, to plan some activity to highlight this issue. But, there was hardly any response. To leave no stone unturned, I even utilised the *myGov* portal, with dismal results. Not discouraged, I also wrote to the Prime Minister, which is reproduced in Annexure-C.

Future need not be as bleak as these disappointing developments point out, thanks to communication technology, competition in the market place and the industries' urge to retain or enhance their market share, social media and the ever increasing awareness among the paying public.

Finally, I always used to ask myself, the fundamental question, especially while taking up important and challenging tasks: "Whether what I am doing is the right thing, which will positively contribute to the end results I am desirous of?" If as per my laid values and understanding my answer is "Yes", then trusting God, I always never looked back and went on to implement the task on hand. Invariably, I was never let down. Every individual has his own value and can definitely play a role for a better tomorrow, provided he is keen to do.

ANNEXURES

Annexure–A

Consumer Protection Council, Rourkela
Consumer Dispute Cases Pursued from 1989 – 2014

Sl. No.	Cause Title	Name of the Court	Case No.	No. of Consumers Represented	Subject	Prayer Allowed /Not Allowed
1	Consumer Protection Council, Rourkela Vs Lohia Machines Ltd., Kanpur	State Commission, Orissa	CD Case No. 48 of 1989	87	Non-refunding of Booking Advance	Allowed
2	Consumer Protection Council, Rourkela Vs Andhra Pradesh Scooters Ltd.	State Commission, Orissa	CD Case No. 49 of 1989	24	Non-refunding of Booking Advance	Allowed
3	Consumer Protection Council, Rourkela Vs Andhra Pradesh Scooters Ltd.	NCDRC	Original Petition No. 29 of 1990	227	Non-refunding of Booking Advance	Allowed
4	Consumer Protection Council, Rourkela Vs Lohia Machines Ltd., Kanpur	NCDRC	Original Petition No. 30 of 1990	1504	Non-refunding of Booking Advance	Allowed

(Contd.)

Sl. No.	Cause Title	Name of the Court	Case No.	No. of Consumers Represented	Subject	Prayer Allowed /Not Allowed
5	Consumer Protection Council, Rourkela Vs Northern Railway & Others	NCDRC	Original Petition No. 17 of 1991	Public Interest	Poor upkeep/ Unhygienic condition of railway compartments	Allowed
6	Consumer Protection Council, Rourkela Vs National Insurance Co. Ltd.	District Forum, Sundergarh	CD Case No. 13 of 1991	1	Non-payment of genuine accident claims.	Not Allowed
7	Consumer Protection Council, Rourkela Vs National Insurance Co. Ltd.	State Commission, Orissa	CD Appeal No. 46 of 1993	1	- do -	Allowed
8	Consumer Protection Council, Rourkela Vs Telecom District Engineer, Rourkela	District Forum, Sundergarh	CD Case No. of 1991	1	Whimsical disconnection of telephone connection	Allowed

Consumer Dispute Cases Pursued ▶ 53

Sl. No.	Cause Title	Name of the Court	Case No.	No. of Consumers Represented	Subject	Prayer Allowed /Not Allowed
9	Consumer Protection Council, Rourkela Vs M/s Gals-N-Dolls, Rourkela	District Forum, Sundergarh-II	CD Case No. of 1991	1	Non-supply of goods, after accepting payment	Allowed
10	Consumer Protection Council, Rourkela Vs M/s Clean India, Rourkela	District Forum, Sundergarh	CD Case No. of 1991	1	Compensation for damaged saree.	Allowed
11	Consumer Protection Council, Rourkela Vs Indian Airlines	NCDRC	Original Petition No. of 1993	Public Interest	Non-specification of fees, for booking tickets by off-line Travel Agents.	Not Allowed
12	Consumer Protection Council, Rourkela Vs Sipani Automobiles, Bangalore	District Forum,-II, Bangalore	CD Case No. of 1993	1	Non-refunding of Booking Advance	Allowed
13	Consumer Protection Council, Rourkela Vs M/s Jilex Finance & Investment Ltd., Calcutta	State Commission, Orissa	CD Case No. 275 of 1993	86	Non-payment of matured policies.	Allowed

(Contd.)

Sl. No.	Cause Title	Name of the Court	Case No.	No. of Consumers Represented	Subject	Prayer Allowed /Not Allowed
4	Consumer Protection Council, Rourkela Vs Rourkela Regional Improvement Trust	NCDRC	First Appeal Nos. 151 to 166 of 1994	14	Can the State Commission allow the Opposite Party itself to decide a dispute?	Allowed
5	Consumer Protection Council, Rourkela Vs GM, South Eastern Railway	District Forum, Sundergarh-II	CD Case No. of 1994	4	Not providing accommodation to passengers, who had confirmed berths.	Allowed
6	Consumer Protection Council, Rourkela Vs Asst. Post Master, Bhubaneswar	District Forum, Sundergarh-II	CD Case No. 26 of 1994	1	Violating terms of NSC Certificates issued, as well as the Gazette Notification	Not Allowed
7	Consumer Protection Council, Rourkela Vs Asst. Post Master, Bhubaneswar	State Commission, Orissa	CD Appeal No. 328 of 1994	1	- do -	Not Allowed

Consumer Dispute Cases Pursued ▶ 55

Sl. No.	Cause Title	Name of the Court	Case No.	No. of Consumers Represented	Subject	Prayer Allowed/Not Allowed
18	Consumer Protection Council, Rourkela Vs Asst. Post Master, Bhubaneswar	NCDRC	Revision Petition No. 1106 of 1995	1	- do -	Not Allowed
19	Consumer Protection Council, Rourkela Vs Sree Shyam Air Services, Rourkela	District Forum, Sundergarh-II	CD Case No. 59 of 1995	1	Non-delivery of the consignment.	Not Allowed
20	Consumer Protection Council, Rourkela Vs Sree Shyam Air Services, Rourkela	State Commission, Orissa	CD Appeal No. 213 of 1996	1	Non-delivery of the consignment.	Allowed
21	Consumer Protection Council, Rourkela Vs Sr. Supdt. Of Post Offices	District Forum, Sundergarh-II	CD Case No. 298/93, Tr. 94/95	2	Unauthorised withdrawals from CTD Accounts	Partially Allowed
22	Consumer Protection Council, Rourkela Vs Sr. Supdt. Of Post Offices	State Commission, Orissa	CD Appeal No. 620 of 1996	2	- do -	Allowed

(Contd.)

Sl. No.	Cause Title	Name of the Court	Case No.	No. of Consumers Represented	Subject	Prayer Allowed /Not Allowed
23	B. Vaidyanathan, Secretary, Consumer Protection Council, Rourkela Vs General Manager, Southern Railway	NCDRC	Original Petition No. 8 of 1995	Public Interest	Whimsical diversion of Bokaro-Alleppey Express, from Chennai Central.	Not allowed (But Railways implemented the Demand)
24	Consumer Protection Council, Rourkela Vs Lucknow Development Authority	District Forum, Lucknow	CD Case No.	1	Non-refund of Booking deposit.	Allowed
25	Consumer Protection Council, Rourkela Vs Rourkela Regional Improvement Trust/Rourkela Development Authority	State Commission, Orissa	CD Case Nos. 336, 338, 345, 346, 350, 353, 354, 358, 360, 362, 364, 365, 366/92 and 182/93	14	Non-providing of infrastructural facilities; violation of Plan and Specifications; delay in handing over possession, etc.	Partially Allowed
26	Consumer Protection Council, Rourkela Vs Rourkela Development Authority	NCDRC	First Appeal Nos. 253-257 of 1998	5	- do -	Allowed

Sl. No.	Cause Title	Name of the Court	Case No.	No. of Consumers Represented	Subject	Prayer Allowed/Not Allowed
27	Consumer Protection Council, Rourkela Vs Indian Oil Corporation Ltd.	State Commission, Orissa	CD Case No. 13 of 1997	Public Interest	Undue delay and stoppage of Home delivery of LPG refills.	Allowed
28	Consumer Protection Council, Rourkela Vs Chairman, Indian Railways & Ors.	NCDRC	Original Petition No. 292 of 1996	Public Interest	After collecting I Class Rail fare, providing II Class Chair Car facility, in Ispat Express.	Not Allowed
29	Consumer Protection Council, Rourkela Vs Chairman, Indian Railways & Ors.	Supreme Court	Civil Appeal 48 of 1999	Public Interest	- do -	Not Allowed (But Railways implemented the Demand)
30	Consumer Protection Council, Rourkela Vs South Eastern Railway	State Commission, Orissa	CD Case No. of 1996	Public Interest	Providing incorrect information by the Railway Enquiry.	Partly Allowed

(Contd.)

Sl. No.	Cause Title	Name of the Court	Case No.	No. of Consumers Represented	Subject	Prayer Allowed /Not Allowed
31	Consumer Protection Council, Rourkela Vs Kalinga & Kalinga Bus Service	District Forum, Sundergarh-II	CD Case No. of 1997	16	Non-completion of journey, due to poor maintenance.	Allowed
32	Consumer Protection Council, Rourkela Vs Principal, St. Paul's School, Rourkela	District Forum, Sundergarh-II	CD Case No. 171 of 1999	1	Non-refunding of fees paid, though the student withdrew much before the commencement of the academic year.	Partly Allowed
33	Consumer Protection Council, Rourkela Vs K.K. & Sons, Rourkela	District Forum, Sundergarh-II	CD Case No. 384 of 1998	1	Failure to comply with Warranty service (mixie).	Allowed
34	Consumer Protection Council, Rourkela Vs Utkal Travels & Tours, Rourkela	District Forum, Sundergarh-II	CD Case No 250 of 1999.	4	Stranded in Andaman, as the Agent misled that the Return flight tickets were also confirmed,	Allowed

Sl. No.	Cause Title	Name of the Court	Case No.	No. of Consumers Represented	Subject	Prayer Allowed /Not Allowed
35	Consumer Protection Council, Rourkela Vs K.K. & Sons, Rourkela	District Forum, Sundergarh-II	Execution Petition No. 22 of 2000	1	For realising the award of Rs. 10,000/- from the OP.	Amount realised.
36	Consumer Protection Council, Rourkela Vs Indian Oil Corporation Ltd. & Ors.	NCDRC	Original Petition No. 224 of 2001	Public Interest	Under-weighment of LPG refills, due to shortcomings in the Bottling Plants, spread across the country.	Allowed
37	In the matter of Authorised Representatives of Parties	NCDRC	Revision Petition No. 1017 of 2002	Public Interest	Whether an Authorised Representative of even a Consumer Organisation can appear and argue in consumer courts or not?	Allowed

(Contd.)

Sl. No.	Cause Title	Name of the Court	Case No.	No. of Consumers Represented	Subject	Prayer Allowed /Not Allowed
38	Consumer Protection Council, Rourkela Vs Fabmall (India) Pvt. Ltd. & Ors.	II Addl. District Forum, Bangalore Urban District	CD Case No. 737 of 2005	1	Supply of damaged Microwave Oven.	Allowed
39	LG Electronics India Pvt. Ltd. Vs Consumer Protection Council, Rourkela	State Commission, Karnataka	CD Appeal No. 793 of 2006	1	The Oven supplied was in order and M/s Fabmall was responsible.	Not Allowed
40	Rourkela Development Authority Vs Consumer Protection Council, Rourkela	Supreme Court	SLP (Civil) 14380/2006	5	The Appellant claimed that the allotments had already been cancelled and NCDRC had not taken note.	Not Allowed

Sl. No.	Cause Title	Name of the Court	Case No.	No. of Consumers Represented	Subject	Prayer Allowed /Not Allowed
41	Consumer Protection Council, Rourkela Vs Indian Oil Corporation Ltd. & Ors.	NCDRC	Review Petition – MA No. 257 of 2007	Public Interest	The Commission had overlooked certain important provisions of the Consumer Protection Act, nor reasons adduced for disallowing.	Not Allowed
42	Consumer Protection Council, Rourkela Vs Indian Oil Corporation Ltd. & Ors.	Supreme Court	Civil Appeal 10126/2010	Public Interest	Failure to invoke certain important provisions of CP Act, relating to loss suffered by the community at large.	Not Allowed

(Contd.)

Sl. No.	Cause Title	Name of the Court	Case No.	No. of Consumers Represented	Subject	Prayer Allowed /Not Allowed
43	Consumer Protection Council, Rourkela Vs Indian Oil Corporation Ltd. & Ors.	Supreme Court	Review Petition (Civil) No. 150 of 2013	Public Interest	The Commission had overlooked certain important provisions of the Consumer Protection Act, nor reasons adduced for disallowing.	Not Allowed
44	Consumer Protection Council, Rourkela Vs Indian Oil Corporation Ltd. & Ors.	Supreme Court	Curative Petition (Civil) No. 84/2014	Public Interest	Failure to invoke certain important provisions of CP Act, relating to loss suffered by the community at large.	Not Allowed

Annexure-B

Letter to the Chief Justice of India

By SPEED POST

Consumer Protection Council, Rourkela (Regd.)
A pioneer in taking up class complaints since 1985
Office of the Chief Mentor
10/18, 40th Street, Nanganallur Chennai-600061. Phone: 044-22241242
E-mail: *vaidya@advantageconsumer.com* Website: *www.advantageconsumer.com*
An aware Consumer is an Asset to the Nation

Ref. No.: CM/SC/IOC/ 18 /2014-15   Date: **14th Jul. 2014**
                                                                             16th

Hon'ble Mr. Justice R.M.Lodha
Chief Justice of India
Supreme Court
NEW DELHI – 110001.

    Sub: Suggestion to change the procedure for considering Curative Petitions.

    Ref : Curative Petition (Civil) No. 84 of 2014, arising out of Review Petition (Civil) No. 150 of 2013 and Civil Appeal No. 10126 of 2010.

Respected Sir,

It is with deep regret that I am placing before you this instance of grave injustice that has been done to the consumer movement in this country.

That the Council (Consumer Protection Council, Rourkela) filed Original Petition No. 224 of 2001, before the National Consumer Disputes Redressal Commission (National Commission) against M/s Indian Oil Corporation Ltd. & Others, for supplying under-weighed LPG refills to the consumers, across the country, with an estimated loss of ₹ 750 crores per year. The Original Petition was necessitated as the said Oil Marketing Company did not own the problem and was not willing to take any action to overcome the said problem created due to the shortcomings in their LPG Bottling Plants. The National Commission agreed with the allegations of the

Page - 1 - of 5

Council, and directed M/s IOC to adopt pre-delivery weighing of the LPG refills, in presence of the consumers, as was prayed by the Council, as an interim measure, commencing from 1st Nov. 2005.

One of the Prayers made before the National Commission, Prayer (d) in the Original Petition was to award 1% of the estimated loss suffered by the consumers to the complainant Council, so that it may utilize for furthering the consumer protection activities. Further, Consumer Protection Act was amended from 15th March 2003, incorporating certain new provisions in "Sec. 14 - Finding of the District Forum", "Sec. 22(2) – Power to Review", among others. The Council accordingly prayed for relief under the new amendments of "Sec. 14(1)(d) – punitive damages", "Sec. 14(1)(hb) – payment of penalty when the goods/services affect large number of consumers" and "Sec. 14(1)(i) – payment of adequate cost" in Jan. 2004 itself and later in writing in April 2004, much before the first interim order was passed in Oct. 2005, relating to steps to be taken for safeguarding the consumers against delivering under-weighed LPG refills.

M/s IOC did not comply with the directives of the National Commission. This was brought to the notice of the National Commission in 2006 as well as in 2007. M/s IOC did accept the violations and the National Commission also took cognizance of the said violations. The National Commission finally passed its order in August 2007 without addressing Prayer (d) of the Complainant and the relief sought under Sec. 14(1)(d), 14(1)(hb) and 14(1)(i). Hence, the Council sought a review under Sec. 22(2), of its Order by the National Commission, in Sept. 2007. Though, the National Commission could have decided the matter by circulation, it had 10 sittings, over a period of about 3 years, and finally said in its order, in July 2010 that the case cannot be re-examined as per the provisions of Sec. 22(2). But, in the said Order, the National Commission did admit that it had not addressed Prayer (d) of the Complainant Council.

Thus after a delay of 1071 days, the Civil Appeal No. 10126 was filed before the Supreme Court, against the final Order, for the non-adjudication of the relief by the National Commission. The bench which heard the matter while condoned the huge delay, termed the appeal as infructuous and dismissed it on 5th Dec. 2012.

The basic question as to why a delay of 1071 days was condoned will obviously demonstrate the glaring error in the judgment. The huge delay was condoned because the Council had sought review of the order of the National Commission for the apparent errors, including but not limited to non-invoking the provision of Sec. 14(1)(hb), etc. of the Consumer Protection Act after having concluded that a large number of consumers were affected by the under-weighed refills delivered by M/s IOC. But the judgment after having observed that the appeal is against the order of the National Commission, has failed to discuss the order in any manner. Instead, the impugned judgment discusses the compliance part of the government and the oil marketing companies, which was not the reason for which the appeal was preferred.

That, in addition to the Statement of the Case, Rejoinder and Supplementary Rejoinder to the Counter Affidavits were filed by the

Appellant, during the course of the hearing and the last one (Additional Supplementary Rejoinder) was not taken on record in spite of the Appellant pleading for allowing him to submit the same on 5th Dec. 2012. In all these documents the Appellant repeatedly prayed for considering the original prayers which were not adjudicated by the National Commission.

In this background, the Judgment of this Hon'ble Court dated 5.12.2012 will glaringly show its total irrelevance to the issues for which this Appellant approached this Hon'ble Court.

The Review sought on the Order, vide Review Petition (Civil) No. 150 of 2013, highlighting the above said glaring shortcomings was also dismissed in Feb. 2013.

Since we were quite confident that the gross miscarriage of justice will be rectified and the consumer movement would be able to start a new chapter in the elimination of Unfair Trade Practices, filed the curative petition (Curative Petition (Civil) No. 84 of 2014). The Petition was duly certified by the learned Shri M.R.Calla, ex-Justice of the Gujarat & Rajasthan High Courts, who is also a designated Sr. Advocate of the Supreme Court. The Certificate provided by him highlights the blatant errors and the miscarriage of justice and natural justice, for which the apex court stands for.

Quoting the **Rupa Ashok Hurra** case, the said Curative Petition has also been rejected.

After having been exposed to the consumer courts and other courts of law for well over 25 years, I have a few humble suggestions to make for your respectful consideration, to prevent national wastage of time, efforts and other resources as well as to save valuable resources of the Hon'ble Supreme Court:

SUGGESTION-1:

1. Since the guidelines provided in the **Rupa Ashok Hurra** case should decide the outcome of the Curative Petitions, as is extensively noticed in all the dismissed Curative Petitions (which account for more than 98%), but for the LGBT Case (Sec. 377 IPC) and the like, procedure for curing major defects in the judgments can be modified.

2. Registry could circulate a format, having two major questions, viz., whether (a) "Hearing" in the case was conducted without due notice – YES/NO and (b) Are you alleging that Member(s) of the Bench which decided the case/passed the judgment had concealed any pecuniary or other interests related with the case – YES/NO.

3. Those who are aggrieved by the Order and the Review thereafter, could be asked to file the format, before the designated Registrar.

4. The Registrar could then decide whether the matter should be looked into by the Judiciary constituted for the purpose.

5. The litigant could place the proof of his allegation, before the Bench constituted for the purpose. Vexatious Petitions could be dealt by the Bench so constituted.

While the litigants will be saved of substantial wastage of resources and the Hon'ble Court will be devoid of botheration to dismiss nearly 98% of the Curative Petitions filed. Thus, the Court will be left with more precious time to attend to other pending cases. After all, a voluntary organisation like ours hardly have any resource even to engage more than one semi-skilled staff on a part-time basis, and the only landline telephone had to be surrendered due to paucity of funds, even after nearly 29 years of service to the community.

SUGGESTION-2:

The Hon'ble Court may also consider allowing the system of Review Petitions only in case of the Government and Government sponsored institutions like the National Commission for Women (NCW) as invariably such Petitions are dismissed straight away, as, may be, the same Bench considers such Review Petitions. This will again minimise the Hon'ble Court's work and is likely to speed up dispensation of justice in other matters.

Let the Act and the Rules remain on paper and we will educate our people to live with that reality.

Respectfully submitted.

With regards,

Yours sincerely,

(B.VAIDYANATHAN) MENTOR
CHIEF MENTOR CONSUMER PROTECTION COUNCIL,
ROURKELA,
NO. 10/18, 40th STREET,
NANGANALLUR, CHENNAI-61

Encl.: Copy of Sr. Advocate, Shri M.R.Calla's Certificate.

Copy to:

1. Hon'ble Mr. Justice H.L.Dattu
   Supreme Court
   New Delhi – 110001.

2. Hon'ble Mr. Justice T.S.Thakur
   Supreme Court
   New Delhi – 110001.

3. Hon'ble Shri Ravi Shankar Prasad
   Union Minister for Law & Justice
   21, Mother Teresa Crescent
   New Delhi – 110011.

Sr. Advocate's Certificate

JUSTICE (Retd.)
High Courts Of Gujarat & Rajasthan

M. R. Calla
Sr. Advocate, Supreme Court of India
Professor Emeritus, National Law University, Jodhpur

V-19, First Floor, Green Park Extension
Gate No. 2, New Delhi-110016
Phone (011) 41660699 Fax: (011) 41660701
Mobile : 9312352729, 9829028453
E-mail : mrcalla@rediffmail.com

78

IN THE SUPREME COURT OF INDIA

CURATIVE JURISDICTION

CURATIVE PETITION NO. _____ OF 2013
IN
REVIEW PETITION (CIVIL) NO.150 OF 2013
(Decided on 12.02.2013)
IN
CIVIL APPEAL NO. 10126 OF 2010
(Decided on 05.12.2012)

[Arising out of the final Judgement and Order dated 16.08.2007 passed by the National Consumer Disputes Redressal Commission at New Delhi in Original Petition No. 224 of 2001 read with the order dated 29.07.2010 passed in Misc. Application No. 257/2007 therein]

IN THE MATTER OF :-

Consumer Protection Council, Rourkela, …PETITIONER
Represented through its Chief Mentor,
Mr. B. Vaidyanathan
10/18, 40th Street, Nanganallur,
CHENNAI- 600 061

VERSUS

Indian Oil Corporation Ltd., represented through
  1) Chairman
     Indian Oil Corporation Ltd.
     Regd. Office: 'Indian Oil Bhawan'
     G-9, Ali Yavar Jung Marg
     Bandra (East)
     MUMBAI- 400 051

- "Ratnam", 15/17, Barwara House, Ajmer Road, **Jaipur**-302 006
- Callas Street, **Jodhpur**
- Paritosh - Krina Calla (Advocates), "Sukoon", Sunrise Park, **Ahmedabad**

Phone : 0141-2222399
Phone : 0291-2640290
Phone : 079-26840078 (R)
Cell : 9825086572 (Krina) 9825025576 (Paritosh)

Justice (Retd.) M. R. Calla
Sr. Advocate, Supreme Court of India
New Delhi

V-19, F.F., Green Park Extn.
New Delhi- 110016
Ph-011-41660699. Fax- 011-41660701
Mob:- 09312352729/ 09829028453
Email-mrcalla@rediffmail.com

2) General Manager (LPG-MO)
Indian Oil Corporation Ltd.
Regd. Office: 'Indian Oil Bhawan'
G-9, Ali Yavar Jung Marg
Bandra (East)
MUMBAI- 400 051

3) Sr. Manager (LPG)
Orissa State Office
Indian Oil Corporation Ltd.
304, Bhoi Nagar, Janpath,
BHUBANESWAR- 751 022

4) Mr. H.S. Dua
Area Manager,
Indian Oil Corporation Ltd. (Marketing Division)
Indane Area Office
Third Floor, Aloke Bharati,
Shahid Nagar
BHUBANESWAR- 751 022

5) Mr. B. Minz
Asst. Manager (LPG)
Indian Oil Corporation Ltd.
HIG-B/19, Phase- III
Chhend
ROURKELA- 769 015

Government of India represented through

6) Director
Legal Metrology
Govt. of India
Deptt. Of Consumer Affairs
Krishi Bhawan
NEW DELHI- 110 001

7) Dy. Director
Legal Metrology
Govt. of India
Deptt. Of Consumer Affairs
Regional Reference Standards

Justice (Retd.) M.R. Calla
Sr. Advocate, Supreme Court of India
New Delhi

V-19, F.F., Green Park Extn.
New Delhi- 110016
Ph-011-41660699. Fax- 011-41660701
Mob:- 09312352729/ 09829028453
Email-mrcalla@rediffmail.com

    Laboratory,
    Khandagiri
    BHUBANESWAR, ORISSA

8) Addl. Secretary
   Deptt. Of Consumer Affairs
   Ministry Of Consumer Affairs And Public
   Distribution
   Krishi Bhawan
   NEW DELHI- 110 001

Government of Odisha represented by

9) The Controller
   Legal Metrology
   Govt. of Odisha
   Food, Supplies And Consumer Welfare
   Department
   BHUBANESWAR

The Local Indane Gas Dealer represented by

10) Secretary
    M/s R.W.C.C.S. Ltd.
    Nanda Bhawan
    Main Road
    ROURKELA- 769 001

AND
Union of India represented by

11) Secretary
    Ministry of Petroleum and Natural Gas
    Govt. of India
    Shashtri Bhawan
    NEW DELHI- 110 001

... RESPONDENTS

Justice (Retd.) M.R. Calla
Sr. Advocate, Supreme Court of India
New Delhi

V-19, F.F., Green Park Extn.
New Delhi- 110016
Ph-011-41660699. Fax- 011-41660701
Mob:- 09312352729/ 09829028453
Email-mrcalla@rediffmail.com

SENIOR ADVOCATE'S CERTIFICATE

1. I have gone through the Curative Petition/ Review Petition, the Civil Appeal and the judgement and order passed by the National Consumer Disputes Redressal Commission at New Delhi read with order in Miscellaneous Application passed by the Commission, and the orders dated 12.02.2013, 05.12.2012, 29.07.2010 and 16.08.2007 respectively passed therein. I have also gone through the pleadings, grounds and the other relevant record made available to me.

2. That having gone through the orders and records mentioned hereinabove as also the law laid down by this Hon'ble Court in the case of Rupa Ashok Hurra vs. Ashok Hurra & Anr. reported in **(2002) 4 SCC 388** and Para 49 to 52 thereof in particular, I certify that :-

   A. The present Curative Petition is not being filed on any of the grounds as mentioned in para 51 of the above judgment. However the present Curative Petition seeks to cure gross miscarriage of justice as is obvious from the grounds set out in the Curative Petition against the order dated 12.02.2013 whereby the Review Petition has been rejected by circulation after the grant of permission on the same date to the petitioner to file the Review Petition by the present petitioner as the Chief Mentor and Authorised Representative of the Consumer Protection Council,

Justice (Retd.) M.R. Calla
Sr. Advocate, Supreme Court of India
New Delhi

V-19, F.F., Green Park Extn.
New Delhi- 110016
Ph-011-41660699, Fax- 011-41660701
Mob:- 09312352729/ 09829028453
Email-mrcalla@rediffmail.com

Rourkela against the order dated 05.12.2012 passed by this Hon'ble Court in the Civil Appeal No. 10126/2010.

B. That it is averred in Para 3 of the Curative Petition that no new grounds have been taken in this Curative Petition and all the grounds mentioned therein had been taken in the Review Petition which was dismissed by Circulation. I find these averments to be correct. I also find from the contents of the Curative Petition that it fulfils the requirements of para 49, 50 and 52 of the judgment of this Hon'ble Court in Rupa Ashok Hurra's case (*supra*).

C. That from the perusal of the judgments, orders and the records made available to me I find that the Consumer Protection Council, Rourkela has been pursuing a common grievance of the Consumers at national level in the matter of under weighing the gas cylinders by the India Oil Corporation Limited as mentioned before the National Consumer Disputes Redressal Commission and to award compensation/damages for the same.

D. That this common grievance of the consumers was based on a survey conducted by the volunteers of the Consumer Protection Council, Rourkela as stated in Para 3.5 of the application made under section 21 of the Consumer Protection Act, 1986 before the National Commission, wherein it was also mentioned on the basis of the surveys that consumers were losing on an average ₹ 24/- per

Justice (Retd.) M.R. Calla
Sr. Advocate, Supreme Court of India
New Delhi

V-19, F.F., Green Park Extn.
New Delhi- 110016
Ph-011-41660699. Fax- 011-41660701
Mob:- 09312352729/ 09829028453
Email-mrcalla@rediffmail.com

refill of Indane as per the prices existing at that time. The Government of India and its concerned functionaries as also the Government of Orissa and the Dealer, i.e., Rourkela Wholesale Consumer Co operative Society (RWCCS) had also been impleaded therein. The prayer made in this Application under section 21 may be perused at Page 79 of the Civil Appeal and the final order passed in the Original Petition No. 224/2001 dated 16.08.2007 is available for perusal at page 1-28 of the Civil Appeal. The operative part of the order dated 16.08.2007 is reproduced as under :-

> "1. The Ministry of Petroleum is given four years time as prayed for, in terms of the submissions and our observations mentioned hereinabove.
>
> 2. The Ministry of Petroleum as well as the Ministry of Consumer Affairs shall ensure that all Marketing Companies do issue necessary instructions that the Distributors will provide to deliveryman proper weighing scale for the purpose of weighing LPG Gas Cylinder in the presence of customers and they will give it due publicity by publishing the same in the vernacular language of each and every state as well as in English and each and every State as well as in English and Hindi newspapers apart from giving similar type of advertisement in TV for information of the consumers."

E. That during the pendency of the Appeal before this Hon'ble Court in response to the orders passed by this Hon'ble Court from time to time, the steps taken by the various Oil Companies to modernise LPG bottling plants and instructions issued by them to the distributors and the directions issued to the dealers so as to ensure

Justice (Retd.) M.R. Calla
Sr. Advocate, Supreme Court of India
New Delhi

V-19, F.F., Green Park Extn.
New Delhi- 110016
Ph-011-41660699. Fax- 011-41660701
Mob:- 09312352729/ 09829028453
Email-mrcalla@rediffmail.com

the carrying of weighing machines by the deliveryman at the time of the delivery of cylinders.

F. That the Appeal was disposed of as in-fructuous in view of the steps taken by the Government of India and the Oil Companies and it was also observed that no further direction was required.

G. That the very reading of the 2nd para of the order dated 05.12.2012 (after the reproduction of the operative part of the order dated 16.08.2007) shows that the matter has been treated as if it was a Special Leave Petition whereas it was a direct Appeal before this Hon'ble Court under section 23 of the Consumer Protection Act, 1986. The very opening of this para is as under :-

"During the pendency of the special leave petition out of which this appeal arises ...."

It was not a case of any Civil Appeal converted as an Appeal after grant of Leave in any Special Leave Petition but a statutory appeal as mentioned hereinabove and it is the trite law that the scope of a statutory appeal is much wider than that of a Special Leave Petition under Article 136 of the Constitution of India.

H. That it is a dismal fact that, yet, in the order under review the Hon'ble Court has felt convinced that the order of which the review

Justice (Retd.) M.R. Calla
Sr. Advocate, Supreme Court of India
New Delhi

V-19, F.F., Green Park Extn.
New Delhi- 110016
Ph-011-41660699. Fax- 011-41660701
Mob:- 09312352729/ 09829028453
Email-mrcalla@rediffmail.com

has been sought does not suffer from any error apparent warranting its reconsideration.

I. That while reviewing the order dated 05.12.2012 it has not been noted that the steps taken by the Government of India and the Oil Companies as mentioned in the order were hardly sufficient to dispose of the Appeal as in-fructuous in view of the prayer made in the application under section 21 because such steps and directions as mentioned in the order were wholly inadequate and incomplete to the relief sought by the Consumer Protection Council, Rourkela. In the order dated 05.12.2012 the Court has referred to the Affidavit filed by Smt. Sushma Rath in August 2012 before this Court. A perusal of this affidavit shows that it is based on the several newspaper cuttings upto the period when the matter was pending before the National Commission and the National Commission had already taken notice of the same. The mention about this material is found upto Para 12 of this affidavit. Before this Hon'ble Court what was deposed by Mrs. Sushma Rath,. contained nothing new and such steps as are mentioned therein were not found to be enough by the National Commission itself. This affidavit virtually amounted to old material in a new bottle and the same had been used before this Hon'ble Court to get the Civil Appeal disposed of as in-fructuous.

Justice (Retd.) M.R. Calla
Sr. Advocate, Supreme Court of India
New Delhi

V-19, F.F., Green Park Extn.
New Delhi- 110016
Ph-011-41660699. Fax- 011-41660701
Mob:- 09312352729/ 09829028453
Email-mrcalla@rediffmail.com

J. That none of the steps or the directions as mentioned in the body of the order dated 05.12.2012 show that the prayer at clause (d) of the application under section 21 of the Consumer Protection Act, 1986 at page 79 of the Civil Appeal have been taken care of and in absence of any such terms or directions or the adjudication of the matter in this regard the Appeal could not be disposed of as infructuous. The adjudication of the grievances with reference to clause (d) at page 79 was all the more necessary because the Consumer Protection Council, Rourkela had sought the review of the order dated 16.08.2007 from the National Commission but the Commission had rejected the review, i.e., M.A. No. 257/2007 on 29.07.2010 by observing with regard to the prayer made in clause (d) which was deemed to have been declined and not maintainable under section 22(2) of the Act with the further observation that it would require a detailed examination of the case which is impermissible under section 22 of the Act and application was dismissed as such while leaving it open to the complainant to have redressal of its grievances as may be permissible under law. Despite a challenge to the order dated 16.08.2007 (with the mention of the order dated 29.07.2010 on the basis of which delay in filing the Appeal had been condoned), the Court had disposed of

9

Justice (Retd.) M.R. Calla
Sr. Advocate, Supreme Court of India
New Delhi

V-19, F.F., Green Park Extn.
New Delhi- 110016
Ph-011-41660699. Fax- 011-41660701
Mob:- 09312352729/ 09829028453
Email-mrcalla@rediffmail.com

the Appeal without any adjudication in this regard and yet in the order dated 12.02.2013 it has been mentioned that the order dated 05.12.2012 does not suffer from any error apparent warranting, reconsideration though it is transparently visible that the order dated 05.12.2012 passed by this Hon'ble Court while disposing of the Statutory Appeal suffers from the vice of non adjudication of the prayer as mentioned herein above, i.e, clause (d) at page 79 of the Civil Appeal.

K. That the impugned orders right from the first order dated 16.08.2007 uptil order which has now been passed by this Hon'ble Court in the Civil Appeal and Review thereof are all oblivious of the amendments which have taken place in the Consumer Protection Act, 1986 since 15.03.2003 to which the reference had been made before the National Commission as well as this Hon'ble Court. The impact of these amendments has been left unnoticed and unadjudicated.

L. That in the above backdrop, a gross miscarriage of justice including the violation of the principles of natural justice has taken place in this case.

Justice (Retd.) M.R. Calla
Sr. Advocate, Supreme Court of India
New Delhi

V-19, F.F., Green Park Extn.
New Delhi- 110016
Ph-011-41660699. Fax- 011-41660701
Mob:- 09312352729/ 09829028453
Email-mrcalla@rediffmail.com

M. That these facts constitute sufficient reasons to entertain this petition seeking reconsideration of order dated 12.02.2013 dismissing the Review Petition (C) No. 150/2013 and the order dated 05.12.2012 passed by this Hon'ble Court in Civil Appeal No. 10126 of 2010.

CERTIFIED ACCORDINGLY

DATE: 18.12.2013
PLACE: NEW DELHI

M.R. CALLA,
Sr. Advocate

JUSTICE (Retd.)
M. R. CALLA, Sr. Advocate
Supreme Court of India
V-19, FF, Green Park Extension
New Delhi-110016

(Reproduced from: *www.advantageconsumer.com*)

Annexure-C

A letter to the Prime Minister

Ref: CM/PM/ 14 /2016-17   Date: 11th June 2016

To

Hon'ble Sri Narendra Modi
Prime Minister of India
South Block,
Raisina Hill,
NEW DELHI – 110011.

Sub: Revitalising the consumer movement and saving the common man.

Respected Sir,

At the outset, we would like to record our deep appreciation for all the efforts that your government has been taking for ensuring a clean, transparent and efficient administration. It is indeed a challenge to put back the economy on its rails, so as to generate investors' confidence and to achieve higher growth and prosperity. The growth of the Indian economy under your stewardship has earned appreciation from all quarters including the developed nations, which indeed gives the hope that the country and its people are in for a bright future.

But the people, especially, the burgeoning middle class, who constitute your core support base, have slowly started feeling the pinch and are feeling let down. The falling interest rates (which is key for the survival of the non-pensioners), increasing taxes and excise duties, with a thrust to reduce the subsidies and increase private stakes are all compounding the financial nightmare of the ordinary people.

We are sure, you are aware that what is best for the USA, can be best here also, provided, we are able to replicate the conditions prevailing therein. For example, even one of the best ministers of your government is found appallingly wanting, to resolve a petty routine issue such as approach to the Velachery MRTS (Mass Rapid Transport System) Railway Station, in Chennai. (Copy of the mail addressed to Hon'ble Sri Suresh Prabhu is attached.)

With a substantial increase in private participation and e-commerce, is the government not keen to strengthen the consumer movement, in the country? Unless we strengthen the systems which are capable of addressing the needs of the people, no wonder will happen.

To elaborate, the consumers/the people were armed with an important piece of legislation, well known as the Consumer Protection Act. The main objective of the Act is to speedily redress the grievances of the consumers, without the frills of the civil court, in different spheres of the domestic life, pertaining to availing of products and services. Irony is, though the Act and the consumer movement started making their presence felt during the 90s, and the Act was even strengthened during the earlier NDA rule (2003), it was with a vengeance deactivated from 2006, by systematically weakening the Central Consumer Protection Council, a nodal consultative body established under the Act. While amending the Act requires the approval of the Parliament, for making changes in the Rules (Central Consumer Protection Rules), the Parliament need not be consulted. Hence, the Ministry (Department of Consumer Affairs, Ministry of Consumer Affairs, Food & Public Distribution) subverted the most important consultative body, envisaged in the Act, to the detriment of the consumer movement and hence the public at large. The constitution of the Central Consumer Protection Council (CCPC) was watered down so much that instead of all the states getting represented in the body, which was the case till 2005, only 4–5 states are to be represented, for a period of 3 years. Which means, the consumer activists, from across the country will get covered only over a period of 24 to 30 years, provided the same states are not represented repeatedly.

It is relevant to note that the consumer movement got a big boost, in the initial phase, say, from 1989 to 1999, mainly because of the Voluntary Organisations, which were working in the field. But these voluntary organisations are now being totally relegated and the consultations have only become a farce.

We had a great hope when your government took over the reins of governance in 2014, but that hope is now slowly turning into a despair. (I was one of those millions who actually supported your candidature for prime ministership, in 2014, though not affiliated to any political party till date.) Our landmark case against M/s Indian Oil Corporation Ltd., against under-weightment of LPG refills, brought relief to crores of housewives across the country, as the Oil Marketing Companies were directed to automate their 184 LPG Bottling Plants, which were found to lack the capability to fill the right quantity of LPG in the refills. Though, the 2003 amended CP Act provides for a penalty of a minimum of 5% of the value of the defective goods/services sold to the consumers, against an estimated value of short-filled refills sold to be of ` 66,500 crores, neither the National Commission (NCDRC) (Original Petition No. 224 of 2001, M.A. No. 257 of 2007), nor the Supreme Court (Curative Petition (Civil) No. 84 of 2014, arising out of Review Petition (Civil) No. 150 of 2013 and Civil Appeal No. 10126 of 2010) had the gumption to deal with this aspect (compensation and penalty) of the case, in spite of filing the Review and Curative Petitions.

As a sad joke, my personal representation through "my Gov", addressed to you in this regard, got referred by an enlightened (!) bureaucrat to the Consumer Coordination Council, New Delhi (an association of consumer groups like ours), of which we are also a Founding Member, and which has never done any litigation.

It is unfortunate that the Ministry of Consumer Affairs and the bureaucrats therein, appear to be neither keen nor having the necessary expertise/wisdom to really play a role for strengthening the consumer movement. Instead, they are keen to introduce amendments to the CP Act, many of which are not going to help; rather, will be a drag on the scarce resources of the government.

Finally, can we expect you to ponder whether promoting the business alone can help, while ignoring the people's need of ensuring that they do get the value for their money, in terms of quality of goods and services? If you do agree with us in our belief that a strong consumer movement (as in the United States) alone can ensure a vibrant business and industry, capable of delivering world class quality products and services, we solicit the following:

1. Immediately amend the Consumer Protection Rules, as it was existing prior to 2005 and pave the way for the meeting of the Central Consumer Protection Council, at least thrice a year;

2. Direct the Department of Consumer Affairs, to file a second Curative Petition, in the Supreme Court, for non-adjudication of an important prayer, in the Civil Appeal No. 10126 of 2010, relating to payment of compensation and penalty; (All the details were shared with the then Additional Secretary, Department of Consumer Affairs, in person, on 30th July 2014. We can share all the details once again, as per requirement.) and

3. Direct the Department of Consumer Affairs to consult the consumer activists, without bias, before placing the proposal for amendments to the Consumer Protection Act.

With warm regards,

Sd./–

(B. VAIDYANATHAN)

CHIEF MENTOR

Encl.: Transcript of our email, ref. no. CM/Rly/119/2014-15, dated 9th Jan. 2015.

(Reproduced from: *Advantage Consumer,* June 2016)

Transcript of our email, ref. no. CM/Rly/119/2014-15

From: B. Vaidyanathan, Chief Mentor

Sent: Saturday, January 10, 2015 12:22 PM

To: Suresh Prabhu Union Minister for Railways

Cc: Suresh Prabhu, Minister for Railways; Suresh Prabhu Minister for Railways

Subject: Fw: Pavement constructed at Velachery Metro Station causing hardhip to rail travellers.

CM/Rly/119/2014-15   9th Jan. 2015

Sir,

As we understand and are being informed that the present government is serious about delivering better governance. But the officials who are working for the government do not seem to be serious about such declared commitments. The Railways appears to be no exception to this general malady affecting India.

The case in point is that in spite of the undersigned's letter dated 4th Sept. 2014, there has been no improvement in the status of the footpath in the last 4 months. Kindly have a look at the 4 attached photographs (Footpath at Velachery MRTS). The footpath constructed at a height of more than 1' above the ground level causes immense hardship to all the physically challenged, women, aged, those suffering from arthritis and those carrying heavy luggage. The designated official to whom the problem was informed is yet to respond. He is designated as Director, Public Grievances only to create "Public Grievances"?

Attached please find some photographs depicting the footpaths laid out at Redmond, Seattle, USA. The whole design (sloping of the footpath to the road level) clearly indicates the care with which such pathways designed to take care of even the physically challenged should be an eye-opener for all those in government and municipal administration. Paving such pathways does not cost anything extra, but reveals the concern you have towards the people who use your facility.

We want India to grow and be comparable with the developed. But dreams will remain a dream and an empty rhetoric if even the officials in responsible positions turn indifferent to such needs in spite of the timely feedback from responsible citizens.

Can we expect some action for making the footpath accessible by one and all?

Shall very much appreciate your reply in confirmation.

Regards,

B. Vaidyanathan
Chief Mentor
Consumer Protection Council, Rourkela
Chennai
Camp: Seattle, US

From: B. Vaidyanathan, Chief Mentor

Sent: Wednesday, September 3, 2014 11:19 PM

To: S.Vijayakumaran, Addl. GM / Director, Public Grievances, Southern Railway

Subject: Pavement constructed at Velachery Metro Station causing hardhip to rail travellers.

CM/SR/46/2014-15   4th Sept. 2014

Sub: Pavement erected at the entrance of Velachery Metro Station causing hardship to rail commuters - especially to the aged, ladies and physically handicapped.

Sir,

Velachery MRTS Station was having free approach from all sides till last month (August 2014). Probably, to prevent crowding of the entrance to the Railway Station, pavements have been laid, that too to a height of about 2 feet, causing inconvenience to the traveling public, especially the aged, handicapped and the ladies, who have to enter the Station (via) the ticket issuing counters. Even others, who can directly board the trains, cannot approach the ramp at the end, without walking through the slush and stagnant water, which is prevailing beyond the pavement, on rainy days.

Railways may consider the following suggestions and implement them urgently, to mitigate the misery of those who are not fully physically fit:

1. Open up the pavement at the front or provide a ramp or small steps, with hand-railings for the people to easily access the Station.

2. Provide a ramp along the hand-railings (which have already been provided) at the entrance to the Railway Station.

3. For regular travelers who can enter the station through the ramps provided, at the platform end, provide a *pucca* (all season) passage way, beyond the pavement.

4. For travelling between the platforms (presently people are crossing the railway lines), provide pavement of about 3 feet wide, to facilitate the passengers walk with more comfort.

Hope, the problems highlighted herein do not need further elucidation. In case, you still need any further visual clarification, I will provide you with photographs of the existing arrangements. I expected the Railways to help the passengers and hence about a fortnight back I contacted 25355793 - the Contact number provided in your website for "Help & Complaints". Unfortunately, till date there is no change in the status and hence this mail.

Shall appreciate your immediate action and a reply in confirmation.

Thanking you,

Yours faithfully,

B. VAIDYANATHAN
Chief Mentor
Consumer Protection Council, Rourkela
Chennai-61.
Website: www.advantageconsumer.com

Annexure-D

Arnab, et al! There are many more vital things other than Sushma bashing! Jago Grahak Jago!!

– B. Vaidyanathan

The media, especially the electronic one, is doing an excellent job in exposing the politicians and their wrong doings. But are they doing the same justice to unknown entities like our Council, which meticulously did its homework and saved crores of unsuspecting housewives from across the country, who were being taken for a ride by the OMCs (Oil Marketing Companies: IOCL, HP & BP) by supplying under-weighed LPG refills? The firm answer is a big NO.

Arnab and their ilk would probably consider the Balance Sheet of the story they are going to carry. Politicians are bashed by everyone and they enjoy not so good esteem among the common man and their TV viewers. So, they will readily gobble it up as a valour which entails all commendation. TRP will go up! All this on the Assets side. While on the Liability side, there is hardly any. Politicians hardly have the time nor the scruples nor the authority to pull up such adventurers, even if they are found to be wrong. Further, the garb of "Freedom of Press" gives them the utmost protection, even when they do not deserve in some cases. *At the same time, this same Press or Media, do they exhibit the same enthusiasm and courage to highlight the shortcomings of the judiciary?* Our experience shows that even in genuine cases, as in ours, the media prefers to remain silent rather than speak the truth and run the risk of earning the displeasure of all powerful judiciary. This is not a good omen for a healthy democracy to flourish.

On 20th July 2013, this author participated in the '*OPEN HOUSE*' organised by '*The Hindu*', rightfully the leader among all the English newspapers, at its headquarters in Chennai, with the noble idea of getting to know the feedback from the readers. During this interaction, this author pointed out the big flaw in the Supreme Court judgement in the LPG (Indane) case had not been published, in spite of the wider ramifications of this case, which involved an estimated loss of over Rs. 65,000 crores to the unsuspecting housewives across the country. Though, the Act provided for imposing a penalty of a minimum of Rs. 3,250 crores on the erring Oil Company (IOCL), Supreme Court preferred not to examine the issues for which the Appeal was preferred by the Council, a voluntary organisation sustaining on meagre resources. Pat came the explanation from the then Editor that even on that date they had published an Editorial against the verdict of the Supreme Court, in the LGBT Case (Lesbians, Gays, Bisexuals and Trans-genders), meaning to say that they are indeed having the gumption and courage to differ from the Supreme Court and are not hesitant to publish the same. Obviously, the newspaper or the media feels comfortable to handle only such legal issues with alacrity which are already highlighted and in the public domain or which helps in garnering more market-share, with least risk. Incidentally, our case story is yet to see the light of the day through this great newspaper, though this author as per the suggestion of the then Editor gave an article for publishing in the "Open Page" of the paper, the next day of the event itself.

Arnab and their ilk, after enjoying the distinction of being one of the pillars of the Indian democracy, do not appear to be too keen to take that role seriously. But they all stand for a new breed of journalism, which is dictated by convenience rather than principles. In our LPG case, to highlight the shortcomings in the Supreme Court verdict, Press was briefed through the **Press Clubs at Chennai, Delhi and Rourkela**. In addition, efforts were taken and journalists of important TV channels, Newspapers, including *Times Now*, *NDTV*, etc. were contacted in person and information shared, with hardly any outcome from such initiatives. It is pertinent to note that we had relentlessly gone up to filing the Curative Petition, to cure the obvious flaws in the SC judgement, but without any tangible results.

When one comes out with "*Lalitgate*", other one comes out with "*Vyapam*" to keep the political soap going, so that their TRPs may not falter and their market-share is retained. Such telecasts are continued for weeks, non-stop, to garner public applause. But why not an "*Indanegate*" or a "*consumergate*" to make a positive contribution to the society. I do not think anybody cares. *They also may not have an inkling that such voluntary efforts unless they are patronised or rewarded appropriately, will meet with a natural death and all the so called special efforts made from time to time by the government and their agencies for invigorating the voluntary movement will tantamount to growing the plantain trees in the desert.*

"Jago Grahak Jago" can be meaningful only when such slogans have a real meaning. After waking up where will he go? To an indifferent government machinery? Or to a casual and whimsical judiciary? Or to an unprincipled media? While all the public ire and media scrutiny is limited to the Legislature, other three enjoy at the cost of a silent society. This does not bode well for a nation seeking to become a super economic power.

(Reproduced from: *Advantage Consumer*, July 2015)

COMMON CAUSE

A REGISTERED SOCIETY

AN ORGANISATION FOR VENTILATING COMMON PROBLEMS OF THE PEOPLE

COMMON CAUSE HOUSE, 5, Institutional Area, Nelson Mandela Road,
Vasant Kunj, New Delhi-110070 • Fax/Phone : 2613-1313

A-31, West End, New Delhi-110021   PH: 26876666

June 27, 2005.

Dear Mr. Vaidyanathan,

    I take this opportunity to convey my great appreciation of the work that Rourkela Branch of the Consumer Movement /has continued to do excellent work all these years. Our grateful thanks are communicated to the Editor and the staff that they collect the information and put together for the regular issue of Advantage Consumer.

    I received the June, 2005 issue for which I convey many thanks.

Kind regards,

Yours sincerely,

(H. D. Shourie)
Director

Mr. B. Vaidyanathan,
Editor,
ADVANATAGE CONSUMER,
Consumer Protection Council, Rourkela
C/66, Sector 2,
ROURKELA - 769 006.
(Orissa)

THE HINDU

News > National
PTI   New Delhi, October 17, 2012 19:26 IST

Ensure LPG consumers are not short-changed, SC fiat to govt

In a boost to consumer rights, the Supreme Court has directed the Union government to ensure that domestic LPG cylinders are checked for their actual weight at the customer's doorstep to avoid any malpractice resorted to by a dealer.

The apex court directive followed an undertaking from the Petroleum and Natural Gas Ministry that instructions will be issued to all oil companies to ensure that in each and every case, the distributor's delivery man carries weighing equipment and the cylinder is delivered to the customer after recording the actual weight of the gas in his/her presence.

A bench of justices G S Singhvi and S J Mukhopadhya also directed the authorities to carry out ads in Doordarshan and other electronic media to create awareness on their rights to measure the weight.

It also said that cylinders should be made in standard specifications so as to ensure that consumers are not misled by different measurements.

"It is important to issue instructions to make people aware. Gas cylinders should be checked and weighed. Government should have addressed this on its own. For years, suppliers have been creating mischief; making money. Earlier these dealerships were a distribution of largesse, a source of earning not service," the bench observed.

The court passed the direction yesterday while dealing with a public interest litigation filed by the Consumer Protection Council through its representative B Vaidyanathan who appeared in person.

The court while agreeing with the petitioner's contention of under-weight of gas in many cases also pointed out that contents and cash memo relating to the weight should be in larger print for the benefit of consumers.

http://www.thehindu.com/news/national/Ensure-LPG-consumers-are-notshort-changed-SC-fiat-to-govt/article12561134.ece

© The Hindu

(Reproduced from: *http://www.thehindu.com*)

(Reproduced from: *Dina Thanthi, Tamil daily, dt. 18.10.2012)*

Inauguration of Council's (delayed) Silver Jubilee (2012)

Meeting the Press at Chennai, after Supreme Court's dismissal, in the LPG case (2013)

www.ingramcontent.com/pod-product-compliance
Lightning Source LLC
Chambersburg PA
CBHW020440220526
45464CB00002B/790